By
Any Means
Necessary

Malcolm X addressing the Militant Labor Forum, New York City, May 29, 1964

By Any Means Necessary

Speeches, Interviews and a Letter by Malcolm X

Edited by George Breitman

A MERIT BOOK

PATHFINDER PRESS, INC.
NEW YORK   1970

A MERIT BOOK

Library of Congress Catalog Card No. 74-108718
Manufactured in the United States of America

The publisher acknowledges with gratitude the permission of the following companies and individuals to use in this book materials by Malcolm X:

Monthly Review, Inc., for "Interview with Malcolm X" by A. B. Spellman, from *Monthly Review*, May, 1964.

Radio Station WLIB, New York, for excerpts from the program "The Editors Speak," broadcast July 4, 1964.

The Militant, for "Letter from Cairo," and "London-to-Paris Interview," from its issues of February 28, 1969, and February 20, 1967, respectively.

Radio Station WMCA, New York (Straus Broadcasting Group, Inc), and Mr. Barry Gray, for excerpts from the Barry Gray Show broadcast November 28, 1964.

Young Socialist for "Interview With Malcolm X," from the March-April, 1965, issue.

CONTENTS

FOREWORD

Most of the story of Malcolm X (born Malcolm Little on May 19, 1925, in Omaha, Nebraska, and assassinated on February 21, 1965, in New York City) was told by Malcolm himself to Alex Haley in 1963 and 1964 for *The Autobiography of Malcolm X* (Grove Press, 1965). The political and ideological aspects of Malcolm's thought in his last year, after he had left the Nation of Islam (Black Muslims) and had set out to build a new movement for black liberation, are presented in the speeches and statements collected in *Malcolm X Speaks* (Merit Publishers, 1965).

By Any Means Necessary is a companion volume to *Malcolm X Speaks*. That is, it contains speeches, interviews and a letter from Malcolm's last year, most of which were not available to the publisher when *Malcolm X Speaks* was prepared. Like the latter, it presents, in Malcolm's own words and with minimal editing, the views that he developed in the final, independent, phase of his life when, as he put it, he was thinking and speaking for himself.

One of the problems encountered in the preparation of *Malcolm X Speaks* was that of repetitions. This arises with anyone who speaks as frequently as Malcolm did; it must also be remembered that, unlike major political candidates in the United States, he had no ghost speechwriters and prepared his talks entirely by himself; in addition, he had the misfortune of being interviewed by reporters who were all too often uninformed, uninterested, or unimaginative. We tried to meet the problem there by omitting repetitious material and indicating the omissions by three periods . . .). The same device is used to avoid repetitions from speech to speech in the present volume and, where possible without affecting the flow of thought or expression, repetitions of material in *Malcolm X Speaks*. (In one chapter we have included the full text of an interview that was only partially used in the earlier collection.)

This seems the appropriate place to clear up a mistaken notion which we may have helped inadvertently to create when we wrote in the foreword to *Malcolm X Speaks* about speeches given "extemporaneously or from brief notes." In his chapter on Malcolm in *Native Sons, A Critical Study of Twentieth-Century Negro American Authors* (J. B. Lippincott Co., 1968), Edward Margolies states it as a "fact that Malcolm never wrote out his speeches before hand but spoke spontaneously from notes." But it is not a fact. Malcolm was capable of speaking brilliantly without notes, or from a brief outline, and often did. But on other occasions, when he had the time to prepare, or considered the talk important, or had new ideas he wanted to express, he carefully wrote out the text of his speech. In this respect he was like W. E. B. Du Bois: he took his audiences seriously, despite his abundant offerings of wit and humor, and felt an obligation to give the best he was capable of. Of course he also felt free to depart from his text and to add suitable or spontaneous material.

Each selection in this book is prefaced by notes reporting the time and place of the speech or interview and calling attention to some of its special or unusual features. Our own interpretations of Malcolm's development after he left the Nation of Islam can be found elsewhere—in *The Last Year of Malcolm X: The Evolution of a Revolutionary* (Merit Publishers, 1967). Here we can only repeat the advice given in *Malcolm X Speaks*: The reader is urged to bear in mind that Malcolm's ideas were developing with rapidity and that certain positions he took in the first two months after his break with the Black Muslims underwent further change in the last months of his life.

George Breitman

AN INTERVIEW
1 BY A. B. SPELLMAN

*Malcolm X did not take the initiative for his departure
from the Nation of Islam which he had worked so hard
to build; Elijah Muhammad, the leader of the sect, did
that by suspending Malcolm indefinitely in December,
1963, ostensibly for an unauthorized remark on the
assassination of President John Kennedy, but actually
because of simmering differences over the role of the
Black Muslims in the developing freedom struggle. During
the three months of his suspension, Malcolm, who had
always been exceptionally loyal and grateful to Muhammad, wrestled with the question of his own role in
the liberation movement. He wanted to remain in the
Nation, but it was clear that Muhammad now distrusted
him and that therefore he was no longer welcome there.
He wanted to play an active part in the black struggle,
but he knew how difficult that would be without a strong
organization through which he could function — and he
was well aware of the work and time the building of
such an organization would require. He had some ideas
about the kind of organization needed, but they were*

1

tentative, incomplete, and untested. And the threats on his life that he began to hear about were not conducive to a leisurely examination and thinking through of those ideas.

Nevertheless, he went ahead. On March 8, 1964, he announced he was leaving the Nation of Islam and starting a new movement, one that would participate in the everyday struggle for "specific objectives" from which the Black Muslims abstained, while at the same time seeking to teach black people that such struggles could not by themselves solve the basic problems. Four days later he held a press conference at which he announced the formation of his new organization, the Muslim Mosque, Inc. One week after that, on March 19, he gave the poet and music critic A. B. Spellman the following interview, which first appeared in Monthly Review, *May, 1964.*

In this interview, and in other statements made during the first months after the split, Malcolm said a number of things about which he later changed his mind. Partly this was because he had not yet had the time to think through certain questions which he had been publicly and automatically answering for years in accordance with the line prescribed by Muhammad. In this category can be placed his statements supporting back-to-Africa separatism and opposing interracial marriage. A few weeks later, by the time he had visited and returned from Mecca and Africa, he changed his mind on separatism, and before his death he said that intermarriage was strictly a personal matter, of concern only to the people directly involved.

Perhaps his remarks to Spellman about white-black solidarity belong in this category too — at least that portion denying the need or usefulness of such solidarity, an orthodox Black Muslim position he had been expressing for over a decade. Intermingled with this long-held position, however, was something new for Malcolm and his closest associates in the Muslim Mosque, Inc.: the view that "there can be no worker solidarity until there's first some black solidarity. There can be no white-

*black solidarity until there's first some black solidarity."
Implied in this was the possibility of white-black solidarity after black solidarity had been achieved. Later
Malcolm explicitly argued that white-black solidarity (on
a militant foundation) was both necessary and de-
sirable— after blacks had organized their own movement.*

*Malcolm changed his opinion about other things he
thought and said at the time of the Spellman interview
because subsequent events and further experience convinced him he had been wrong. Here and in the first
period of the split he continued to praise Muhammad,
hoping in this way to avoid a bitter struggle that he
had no interest in pursuing; he wanted to turn outward,
away from sectarian narrowness and toward the organization of the millions of non-Muslim blacks. But Muhammad would not have it that way, and Malcolm later
said his conciliatory tactic had been a mistake. He also
realized that his major objective— the unification of the
non-Muslim black masses into a militant movement—
had been hampered rather than advanced by his first
organizational step, the formation of a* Muslim *group.
So he soon restricted the Muslim Mosque, Inc., to a
primarily religious role, and created another, secular,
organization.*

*Most of those who criticized such changes as evidence
that Malcolm was "floundering" or "unstable" either did
not understand what Malcolm was trying to do and the
difficulty of doing it, or they understood it very well
but did not want others to understand it. Misunderstand-
ing and malice have long been the lot of revolutionaries.*

A. B. Spellman: Please answer these charges that are
often raised against you: That you are as racist as
Hitler and the Klan, etc. That you are anti-Semitic.
That you advocate mob violence.

Malcolm X: No, we're not racists at all. Our brotherhood is based on the fact that we are all black, brown,
red, or yellow. We don't call this racism, any more than
you could refer to the European Common Market, which

consists of Europeans, which means that it consists of white-skinned people—is not referred to as a racist coalition. It's referred to as the European Common Market, an economic group, while our desire for unity among black, brown, red, and yellow is for brotherhood—has nothing to do with racism, has nothing to do with Hitler, has nothing to do with the Klan. In fact, the Klan in this country was designed to perpetuate an injustice upon Negroes whereas the Muslims are designed to eliminate the injustice that has been perpetuated upon the so-called Negro.

We're antiexploitation, and in this country the Jews have been located in the so-called Negro community as merchants and businessmen for so long that they feel guilty when you mention that the exploiters of Negroes are Jews. This doesn't mean that we are anti-Jews or anti-Semitic—we're antiexploitation.

No. We have never been involved in any kind of violence whatsoever. We have never initiated any violence against anyone, but we do believe that when violence is practiced against us we should be able to defend ourselves. We don't believe in turning the other cheek.

Spellman: Why did you find it necessary to split with the Nation of Islam?

Malcolm: Well, I did encounter opposition within the Nation of Islam. Many obstacles were placed in my path, not by the Honorable Elijah Muhammad, but by others who were around him, and since I believe that his analysis of the race problem is the best one and his solution is the only one, I felt that I could best circumvent these obstacles and expedite his program better by remaining out of the Nation of Islam and establishing a Muslim group that is an action group designed to eliminate the same ills that the teachings of the Honorable Elijah Muhammad have made so manifest in this country.

Spellman: What is the name of the organization that you have founded?

Malcolm: The Muslim Mosque, Inc., which means we are still Muslims—we still worship in a mosque and we're incorporated as a religious body.

Spellman: Can other Muslims work with the Muslim Mosque, Inc., without leaving the Nation of Islam?

Malcolm: Oh yes. Yes, anyone who is in the Nation of Islam who wants to work with us and remain in the Nation of Islam, is welcome. I am a follower of the Honorable Elijah Muhammad — I believe in the Honorable Elijah Muhammad. The only reason I am in the Muslim Mosque, Inc., is because I feel I can better expedite his program by being free of the restraint and the other obstacles that I encountered in the Nation.

Spellman: Will you have access to *Muhammad Speaks?*

Malcolm: Probably not. No, I very much doubt that the same forces which forced me out would permit me access to the *Muhammad Speaks* newspaper as an organ, although I am the founder of the paper, the originator of the paper. Few people realize it — I was the one who originated *Muhammad Speaks* newspaper. The initial editions were written entirely by me in my basement.

Spellman: Will you start another publication?

Malcolm: Yes. One of the best ways to propagate any idea is with a publication of some sort, and if Allah blesses us with success we will have another publication. We'll probably name it the *Flaming Crescent* because we want to set the world on fire.

Spellman: How religious is the Muslim Mosque, Inc.? Will it be more politically oriented?

Malcolm: The Muslim Mosque, Inc., will have as its religious base the religion of Islam, which will be designed to propagate the moral reformation necessary to up the level of the so-called Negro community by eliminating the vices and the other evils that destroy the moral fiber of the community — this is the religious base. But the political philosophy of the Muslim Mosque will be black nationalism, the economic philosophy will be black nationalism, and the social philosophy will be black nationalism. And by political philosophy I mean we still believe in the Honorable Elijah Muhammad's solution as complete separation. The 22 million so-called Negroes should be separated completely

from America and should be permitted to go back home
to our African homeland, which is a long-range program. So the short-range program is that we must eat
while we're still here, we must have a place to sleep,
we must have clothes to wear, we must have better jobs,
we must have better education. So that although our
long-range political philosophy is to migrate back to
our African homeland, our short-range program must
involve that which is necessary to enable us to live a
better life while we are still here. We must be in complete
control of the politics of the so-called Negro community;
we must gain complete control over the politicians in
the so-called Negro community, so that no outsider will
have any voice in the so-called Negro community. We'll
do it ourselves.

Spellman: Whom do you hope to draw from in organizing this political movement—what kind of people?

Malcolm: All—we're flexible—a variety. But our accent will be upon youth. We've already issued a call
for the students in the colleges and universities across
the country to launch their own independent studies of
the race problem in the country and then bring their
analyses and their suggestions for a new approach back
to us so that we can devise an action program geared
to their thinking. The accent is on youth because the
youth have less stake in this corrupt system and therefore can look at it more objectively, whereas the adults
usually have a stake in this corrupt system and they
lose their ability to look at it objectively because of their
stake in it.

Spellman: Do you expect to draw from the Garveyite
groups?

Malcolm: All groups—Nationalist, Christians, Muslims,
agnostics, atheists, anything. Everybody who is interested
in solving the problem is given an invitation to become
actively involved with either suggestions or ideas or something.

Spellman: Will the organization be national?

Malcolm: National? I have gotten already an amazing
number of letters from student groups from college cam-

puses from across the country expressing a desire to
become involved in a united front in this new idea that
we have.

Spellman: What kind of coalition do you plan to make?
Can whites join the Muslim Mosque, Inc.?

Malcolm: Whites can't join us. Everything that whites
join that Negroes have they end up out-joining the Negroes. The whites control all Negro organizations that
they can join—they end up in control of those organizations. If whites want to help us financially we will accept
their financial help, but we will never let them join us.

Spellman: Then black leadership is necessary?

Malcolm: Absolutely black leadership.

Spellman: Will you work with the so-called "established"
civil rights organizations?

Malcolm: Well, we will work with them in any area
and on any objective that doesn't conflict with our own
political, economic, and social philosophy, which is black
nationalism. I might add that I was invited to attend a
civil rights group meeting where all of the various civil
rights organizations were present and I was invited to
address them in Chester, Pennsylvania. Gloria Richardson was there; Landry, the head of the Chicago school
boycott, was there; Dick Gregory was there; many others
were there; the Rochedale movement was there. Now my
address to them was designed to show them that if they
would expand their civil rights movement to a human
rights movement, it would internationalize it. Now, as
a civil rights movement, it remains within the confines
of American domestic policy and no African independent
nations can open up their mouths on American domestic affairs; whereas if they expanded the civil rights movement to a human rights movement then they would be
eligible to take the case of the Negro to the United Nations, the same as the case of the Angolans is in the
UN and the case of the South Africans is in the UN.
Once the civil rights movement is expanded to a human
rights movement, our African brothers and our Asian
brothers and our Latin American brothers can place
it on the agenda at the General Assembly that is coming

up this year, and Uncle Sam has no more say-so in it then. And we have friends outside the UN — 700 million Chinese who are ready to die for human rights.

Spellman: Do you intend to collaborate with such other groups as labor unions or socialist groups or any other groups?

Malcolm: We will work with anybody who is sincerely interested in eliminating injustices that Negroes suffer at the hands of Uncle Sam.

Spellman: What is your evaluation of the civil rights movement at this point?

Malcolm: It has run its — it's at the end of its leash.

Spellman: What groups do you consider most promising?

Malcolm: I know of no group that is promising unless it's radical. If it's not radical, it is in no way involved effectively in the present struggle.

Spellman: Some local civil rights leaders have said they'd welcome your support, some national leaders have said they want nothing to do with you: what is your reaction?

Malcolm: Well, the local civil rights leaders are usually involved right in the midst of the situation. They see it as it is and they realize that it takes a combination of groups to attack the problem most effectively and, also, most local civil rights leaders have more independence of action and usually they are more in tune and in touch with the people. But the national leaders of the civil rights movement are out of touch with the problem and usually they are paid leaders. The local leaders usually have a job and they lean against the local situation on the side, but the nationally known leaders are paid. They are full-time leaders, they are professional leaders and whoever pays their salary has a great say-so in what they do and what they don't do. So naturally the ones who pay the salaries of these nationally known Negro leaders are the white liberals, and white liberals are shocked and frightened whenever you mention anything about some X's.

Spellman: What is your attitude toward Christian-Gandhian groups?

Malcolm: Christian? Gandhian? I don't go for any-

thing that's nonviolent and turn-the-other-cheekish. I don't
see how any revolution — I've never heard of a nonviolent revolution or a revolution that was brought about
by turning the other cheek, and so I believe that it is
a crime for anyone to teach a person who is being brutalized to continue to accept that brutality without doing
something to defend himself. If this is what the Christian-
Gandhian philosophy teaches, then it is criminal — a
criminal philosophy.

Spellman: Does the Muslim Mosque, Inc., oppose integration and intermarriage?

Malcolm: We don't have to oppose integration because
the white integrationists themselves oppose it. Proof of
which, it doesn't exist anywhere where white people say
they are for it. There's just no such thing as integration
anywhere, but we do oppose intermarriage. We are as
much against intermarriage as we are against all of
the other injustices that our people have encountered.

Spellman: What is the program for achieving your
goals of separation?

Malcolm: A better word to use than separation is independence. This word separation is misused. The thir-
teen colonies separated from England but they called it
the Declaration of Independence; they don't call it the
Declaration of Separation, they call it the Declaration
of Independence. When you're independent of someone
you can separate from them. If you can't separate from
them it means you're not independent of them. So, your
question was what?

Spellman: What is your program for achieving your
goals of independence?

Malcolm: When the black man in this country awakens,
becomes intellectually mature and able to think for himself, you will then see that the only way he will become
independent and recognized as a human being on the
basis of equality with all other human beings, he has
to have what they have and he has to be doing for himself what others are doing for themselves. So the first
step is to awaken him to this, and that is where the
religion of Islam makes him morally more able to rise
above the evils and the vices of an immoral society.
And the political, economic, and social philosophy of

black nationalism instills within him the racial dignity and the incentive and the confidence that he needs to stand on his own feet and take a stand for himself.

Spellman: Do you plan to employ any kind of mass action?

Malcolm: Oh, yes.

Spellman: What kinds?

Malcolm: We'd rather not say at this time, but we definitely plan to employ mass action.

Spellman: How about the vote—will the Muslim Mosque, Inc., run its own candidates or support other candidates?

Malcolm: Since the political structure is what has been used to exploit the so-called Negroes, we intend to gather together all of the brilliant minds of students—not the adult politicians who are part of the corruption but the students of political science—we intend to gather all of them together and get their findings, get their analyses, get their suggestions, and out of these suggestions we will devise an approach that will enable us to attack the politicians and the political structure where it hurts the most, in order to get a change.

Spellman: If the Muslim Mosque, Inc., joined in a demonstration sponsored by a nonviolent organization, and whites countered with violence, how would your organization react?

Malcolm: We are nonviolent only with nonviolent people. I'm nonviolent as long as somebody else is nonviolent—as soon as they get violent they nullify my nonviolence.

Spellman: A lot of leaders of other organizations have said they would welcome your help but they qualify that by saying "if you follow our philosophy." Would you work with them under these circumstances?

Malcolm: We can work with all groups in anything but at no time will we give up our right to defend ourselves. We'll never become involved in any kind of action that deprives us of our right to defend ourselves if we are attacked.

Spellman: How would the Muslim Mosque, Inc., handle a Birmingham, Danville, or Cambridge—what do you think should have been done?

Malcolm: In Birmingham, since the government has proven itself either unable or unwilling to step in and find those who are guilty and bring them to justice, it becomes necessary for the so-called Negro who was the victim to do this himself. He would be upholding his constitutional rights by so doing, and Article 2 of the Constitution—it says concerning the right to bear arms in the Bill of Rights: "A well-regulated militia being necessary to the security of a free state, the right of the people to keep and bear arms shall not be infringed." Negroes don't realize this, that they are within their constitutional rights to own a rifle, to own a shotgun. When the bigoted white supremists realize that they are dealing with Negroes who are ready to give their lives in defense of life and property, then these bigoted whites will change their whole strategy and their whole attitude.

Spellman: You've said this will be the most violent year in the history of race relations in America. Elaborate.

Malcolm: Yes. Because the Negro has already given up on nonviolence. This new-thinking Negro is beginning to realize that when he demonstrates for what the government says are his rights, then the law should be on his side. Anyone standing in front of him reclaiming his rights is breaking the law. Now, you're not going to have a lawbreaking element inflicting violence upon Negroes who are trying to implement the law, so that when they begin to see this, like this, they are going to strike back. In 1964 you'll find Negroes will strike back. There never will be nonviolence anymore, that has run out.

Spellman: What is your evaluation of Monroe?

Malcolm: I'm not too up on the situation in Monroe, North Carolina. I do know that Robert Williams became an exile from this country simply because he was trying to get our people to defend themselves against the Ku Klux Klan and other white supremist elements, and also Mae Mallory was given twenty years or something like

that because she was also trying to fight the place of
our people down there. So this gives you an idea of
what happens in a democracy — in a so-called democracy — when people try to implement that democracy.

Spellman: You often use the word revolution. Is there
a revolution underway in America now?

Malcolm: There hasn't been. Revolution is like a forest
fire. It burns everything in its path. The people who are
involved in a revolution don't become a part of the
system — they destroy the system, they change the system.
The genuine word for a revolution is *Umwaelzung* which
means a complete overturning and a complete change,
and the Negro revolution is no revolution because it
condemns the system and then asks the system that it
has condemned to accept them into their system. That's
not a revolution — a revolution changes the system, it
destroys the system and replaces it with a better one.
It's like a forest fire, like I said — it burns everything
in its path. And the only way to stop a forest fire from
burning down your house is to ignite a fire that you
control and use it against the fire that is burning out
of control. What the white man in America has done,
he realizes that there is a black revolution all over the
world — a nonwhite revolution all over the world — and
he sees it sweeping down upon America. And in order
to hold it back he ignited an artificial fire which he has
named the Negro revolt, and he is using the Negro
revolt against the real black revolution that is going
on all over this earth.

Spellman: Can the race problem in America be solved
under the existing political-economic system?

Malcolm: No.

Spellman: Well then, what is the answer?

Malcolm: It answers itself.

Spellman: Can there be any revolutionary change in
America while the hostility between black and white working classes exists? Can Negroes do it alone?

Malcolm: Yes. They'll never do it with working class
whites. The history of America is that working class
whites have been just as much against not only working

class Negroes, but *all* Negroes, period, because all Negroes are working class within the caste system. The
richest Negro is treated like a working class Negro.
There never has been any good relationship between the
working class Negro and the working class whites. I
just don't go along with — there can be no worker solidarity until there's first some black solidarity. There can
be no white-black solidarity until there's first some black
solidarity. We have got to get our problems solved first
and then if there's anything left to work on the white
man's problems, good, but I think one of the mistakes
Negroes make is this worker solidarity thing. There's
no such thing — it didn't even work in Russia. Right
now it was supposedly solved in Russia but as soon
as they got their problems solved they fell out with China.

Spellman: Will the Muslim Mosque, Inc., identify with
nonwhite revolutionary movements in Africa, Asia, and
Latin America?

Malcolm: We are all brothers of oppression and today
brothers of oppression are identified with each other all
over the world.

Spellman: Is there anything else you want to say?

Malcolm: No. I've said enough — maybe I've said too
much.

ANSWERS TO
QUESTIONS AT THE
2 MILITANT LABOR FORUM

Malcolm X Speaks *contains a formal speech on "The Black Revolution" given by Malcolm X on April 8, 1964, at a meeting sponsored by the Militant Labor Forum at Palm Gardens in New York. Overlooked at the time was the informal question and answer period following the speech, which fortunately was preserved on tape and is here printed for the first time. Most of the twenty-one questions from the audience could not be clearly distinguished on the tape, and are indicated only by a phrase, except when they were submitted in writing.*

The chairman of the meeting was Richard Garza, who turned the chair over to Malcolm during the question period, so that Malcolm called for the questions in addition to answering them. It was Garza whom Malcolm contrasted with the twenty-first speaker, whose "question" turned out to be a denunciation of Malcolm as "bloodthirsty" and a lecture on what was wrong with his views. The audience was about three-quarters white, a mixture of radicals who responded favorably to Malcolm's remarks and liberals who were shocked or offended by his forthrightness.

The Freedom Now Party (Questions 2 and 3) was a pioneer effort to build a nationwide black political party.

Launched in 1963, it developed a number of branches in the North in 1964; but the only place where it won statewide ballot status was Michigan. Although Malcolm said he did not know much about the Freedom Now Party in April, when he was in Africa in September he gave serious consideration to the offer of the Michigan party leaders to run him as its candidate for the United States Senate in November. (He would have broken no precedents for changing his residence; that was the year Robert F. Kennedy of Massachusetts chose to become a Senator—from New York.) After thinking it over, however, Malcolm felt compelled to decline the offer with thanks because his schedule in Africa would not permit his return to the United States until after the November election. The Freedom Now Party disintegrated after the election.

Malcolm spoke three times at the Militant Labor Forum during his last year, and maintained friendly relations with the socialist weekly, The Militant, *which was the only paper, white or black, that supported and publicized what Malcolm was trying to do after he left the Black Muslims.*

Question 1: (about the accuracy of *The Militant*)

Malcolm X: I've never found any misquote in *The Militant* of us, and I think any white newspaper, and I guess that's what it is, that can quote a black man correctly is certainly a militant newspaper.

Question 2: (about school integration and the Freedom Now Party)

Malcolm: If I understood you correctly you asked two questions: Number one— am I in favor of integration in the public schools? And number two— am I in favor of the Freedom Now Party?

Insofar as integration in the public schools is concerned, I don't know anywhere in America where they have an integrated school system, North or South. If they don't have it in New York City, they definitely never will have it in Mississippi. And anything that won't work I'm not in favor of. Anything that's not practical I'm not in favor of.

This doesn't mean I'm for a segregated school system. We are well aware of the crippled minds that are produced by a segregated school system, and when Rev. [Milton] Galamison was involved in a boycott against this segregated school system, we supported it. This doesn't make me an integrationist, nor does it make me believe that integration is going to work; but Galamison and I agree that a segregated school system is detrimental to the academic diet, so-called diet, of the children who go to that school.

But a segregated school system isn't necessarily the same situation that exists in an all-white neighborhood. A school system in an all-white neighborhood is not a segregated school system. The only time it's segregated is when it is in a community that is other than white, but at the same time is controlled by the whites. So my understanding of a segregated school system, or a segregated community, or a segregated school, is a school that's controlled by people other than those that go there.

But in an all-white neighborhood, where you have an all-white school, that's not a segregated school. Usually they have a high-caliber education. Anytime someone else can put on you what they want, naturally you're going to have something that's inferior. So the schools in Harlem are not controlled by the people in Harlem, they're controlled by the man downtown. And the man downtown takes all of the tax dollars and spends them elsewhere, but he keeps the schools, the school facilities, the schoolteachers, and the schoolbooks, material, in Harlem at the very lowest level. So this produces a segregated education, which doesn't do our people any good.

On the other hand, if we can get an all-black school, that we can control, staff it ourselves with the type of teachers that have our good at heart, with the type of books that have in them many of the missing ingredients that have produced this inferiority complex in our people, then we don't feel that an all-black school is necessarily a segregated school. It's only segregated when it's controlled by someone from outside. I hope I'm making my point. I just can't see where if white people can go to a white classroom and there are no Negroes present and it doesn't affect the academic diet they're receiving, then I don't see where an all-black classroom can be affected by the absence of white children. If the absence of black children doesn't affect white students, I don't see how the absence of whites is going to affect the blacks.

So, what the integrationists, in my opinion, are saying, when they say that whites and blacks must go to school together, is that the whites are so much superior that just their presence in a black classroom balances it out. I can't go along with that. Yes, ma'am?

Question 3: (again about the Freedom Now Party)

Malcolm: The Freedom Now Party — I don't know too much about it, but what I know about it, I like.

Question 4: (about whites too being hurt by Congressional filibusters)

Malcolm: If I understood you correctly, you were saying that those white senators and congressmen there that are filibustering and other things have done whites as much harm as they've done blacks. I just can't quite go along with that. You see, it's the black man who sits on the hot stove. You might stand near it but you don't sit on it.

Questions 5 and 6: (in writing — about white radicals and African misleaders)

Malcolm: A question sent up: "Can black people achieve their freedom without the help of white radicals, who have more experience at fighting?" And the second question is — this is from a real white liberal — "Some black leaders, even in Africa, are misleading their people," and he says, "I mean Nasser too." I know this is from a liberal. I can even tell what geographic area he's from.

In regard to the first question — Can black people achieve their freedom without the help of white radicals, who have more experience at fighting? — all of the freedom that white people have gotten in this country and elsewhere: they haven't gotten it just fighting themselves. You've always had someone else to do your fighting for you. You perhaps haven't realized it. England became powerful because she had others to fight for her. She used the African against the Asian and the Asian against the African. France used the Senegalese. All these white powers have had some little lackeys to do their fighting for them, and America has had 22 million African-Americans to do your fighting for you.

It is we who have fought your battles for you, and have picked your cotton for you. We built this house that you're living in. It was our labor that built this house. You sat beneath the old cotton tree telling us how long to work or how hard to work, but it was our labor, our sweat and our blood that made this country what it is, and we're the only ones who haven't benefited from it. All we're saying today is, it's payday— retroactive.

And where this gentleman said some black leaders in Africa also mislead their people, I guess you're talking about black leaders like Tshombe, but not — One of the greatest black leaders was Lumumba. Lumumba was the rightful ruler of the Congo. He was deposed with American aid. It was America, the State Department of this country, that brought Kasavubu to this country, interceded for him at the UN, used its power to make certain that Kasavubu would be seated as the rightful or recognized ruler of the Congo. And as soon as Kasavubu, with American support, became the ruler of the Congo, he went back to the Congo, and his first act upon returning home was to turn Lumumba over to Tshombe. So you can easily see whose hand it was behind the murder of Lumumba. And chickens come home to roost.

And then you mention Nasser. Well, I think that's a subjective, subconscious reaction on your part, the fact that you included Nasser's name— I know who you are. Before the Egyptian revolution, Farouk was a monarch in Egypt who had exploited the people with the aid of the West. Naguib and Nasser brought about a revo-

lution, and those who have visited the African continent
today will tell you, if they are objective in their observa-
tions, that Egypt is one of the most highly industrialized
nations on the African continent — the only other nation
is a white nation and that's South Africa. But under
Nasser the Egyptians have become a highly industrialized nation; they're trying to elevate the standard of living of their people.

You'll find that there's a tendency in the West to have
the attitude toward any African leader who has the mass
support of his people — usually the West classifies him
as a dictator. And I can name them. Nkrumah is called
a dictator because he has his people with him; Nasser
is called a dictator, Ben Bella is a dictator, Sékou Touré
is called a dictator — all of these people who are called
dictators by the West usually are classified by the West
as anti-West, because the West can't tell them what to do.
Yes, ma'am?

Question 7: (about going to the United Nations)

Malcolm: And this is one of the reasons why — the
lady asked do we have any feasible plan of bringing
this fight to the UN. The very fact that there has been
a civil rights struggle, since 1954 actually, and at no
time have any of the Negro civil rights leaders made
any effort to take it before the United Nations — that
right there should give you a hint that there's a conspiracy involved. When every other underdog on this
earth — I mean some of the underdogs way out in the
South Pacific — have had their plight taken to the UN;
people who don't even know where the UN is — still the
UN is arguing about their situation. And here we have
22 million black people *surrounding* the UN, and nothing concerning their plight is taken to the UN. Don't
tell me that it's not an atrocity. Any time a church is
bombed — there's no more outright example of the vio-
lation of human rights than when you are sitting in
church and have it bombed, and four little black babies
are murdered. And [when] that still doesn't reach the
UN, then I say there's a conspiracy.

So our contention is that the white liberals, so-called
liberals, infiltrated the civil rights movement, and got

the black people barking up the wrong tree. Because
white people are intelligent enough to know that the
problem will never be solved in Washington, D. C. There
are crooks there, but you can take the crooks who are
in Washington, D. C., downtown before the world court.
If they know that you can take them to court, they'll
start acting right. That's the only time they'll act right.
And then they won't be acting right because they believe
in legality or morality or anything like that—they have
none of that in them. They'll only be acting right because they don't want you to take them to court.

So, yes, there's a machinery being set up right now.
And many of our brothers and sisters from Africa and
Asia and in other parts of this earth, whose nations
have emerged and become independent, are capable and
well qualified to lend all of the support at their disposal
to the problem of the black people in this country, once
it gets into the UN. But they cannot become involved
in it as long as it's called a civil rights struggle — because protocol keeps them from becoming involved in
any of America's domestic affairs. Civil rights is domestic. Human rights is international.

Now, if you consider yourself a true liberal—and me,
I haven't found one. When I say that, I'm bearing in
mind I haven't met all white people, but among those
that I've met I haven't met one yet that would pass the
test; I might meet somebody else tomorrow—

[James Wechsler, *New York Post* editor, takes floor
and begins to speak before being called on.]

Sir, "What do we do about the minister?" Why didn't
you put up your hand and wait until I called on you?
No, why didn't you find out? Why didn't you put up
your hand till I called on you? You're being rude. You're
proving my point. [*Calls on someone else.*] Yes, sir?

Question 8: (about Karl Marx, imperialism, and automation)

Malcolm: Number one, I don't know too much about
Karl Marx. That's number one—I just don't know too
much about Karl Marx. However, it is true that when
a nation loses its markets, no matter how capitalistic
or highly industrialized it is or how much goods it can

produce, when it loses those markets, it's in trouble. And this is one of the basic factors behind America's problem. She has lost her world markets. It's not just automation that's putting her out, giving her a headache. She has no markets. There was a time when the whole world was her market. But today she's hated. Not only is she losing her markets because she's hated, but the European nations are industrialized — they can produce goods cheaper than America can. Japan produces goods cheaper than she and undersells her. And the nations of Africa and Asia would rather buy their manufactured or finished products from other than America.

So it is not so much that automation is causing the unemployment situation — which affects the Negro first and foremost because he's the last hired and has to be the first fired. But it's just the fact that America has run out of markets. And it is impossible for her to find new markets anywhere, unless there's some customers on the moon or on some other planet. And as long as this situation exists, America's economy is going to continue to go down, her dollar will continue to lose its value, and when her dollar loses its value she's lost all her friends. Because the only friends she has are those whom she has bought.

And one further comment is this: as I said, I don't know too much about Karl Marx, but there was this man who wrote *The Decline of the West*, Spengler — he had another book that's a little lesser known, called *The Hour of Decision*. In fact, someone gave me the book out in front of this place one night, a couple of years ago, because I had never heard of it either. I imagine it might be someone who's in this audience or who had that type of thinking. It was at a meeting like this.

And in Spengler's *Hour of Decision*, it's about world revolution, and his thesis is that the initial stages of the world revolution would make people be forced to line up along class lines. But then after a while the class lines would run out and it would be a lineup based upon race. Well, I think he wrote this in the early thirties. And it has actually taken place. Even when the United Na-

tions was put together, the blocs were divided up along
class or some kind of economic philosophy. But today
the blocs that exist in the UN are based on race, along
color lines. You have your Arab-Afro-Asian bloc — they
are all black, brown, red, or yellow. You have your
other blocs and your other blocs, but when you find
those blocs you usually find everybody in them has
something in common and the most that they have in
common usually is the color of their skin, or the absence of color from their skin. Yes, sir?

Question 9: (about the role of whites)

Malcolm: Well, if you noticed when I was speaking I
said the whites can help, if they're progressive-minded.
But my observation and analysis of the kind of help
they've been giving makes me very cautious about the
help that they offer. And I say that because of this: as
I said, I grew up with whites. Most of them are intelligent. At least they used to be. No white person would
go about fighting for freedom in the same manner that
he has helped me and you to fight for our freedom. No,
none of them would. When it comes to black freedom,
then the white man freedom-rides and sits in, he's nonviolent, he sings "We Shall Overcome" and all that stuff.
But when the property of the white man himself is threatened, or the freedom of the white man is threatened, he's
not nonviolent. He's only nonviolent when he's on your
side. But when he's on his side he loses all that patience
and nonviolence.

So, if the whites are sincere in this struggle they will
show the black man how to employ or use better tactics,
tactics that will get results — and not results a hundred
years from now. Our people aren't going to wait ten
years. If this house is a house of freedom and justice
and equality for all, if that's what it is, then let's have
it. And if we can't all have it, none of us will have it.

Question 10: (in writing — about the ballot)

Malcolm: Question: "Do you really think the Negro
can win with the ballot? If not, why not?"

The Negro in this country, before he can win with the
ballot, has to be made more politically mature. Now

many Negroes don't like to be criticized — they don't like for it to be said that we're not ready. They say that that's a stereotype. We have assets — we have liabilities as well as assets. And until our people are able to go in a closet, put you out, and analyze ourselves and discover our own liabilities as well as our assets, we never will be able to win any struggle that we become involved in. As long as the black community and the leaders of the black community are afraid of criticism and want to classify all criticism, collective criticism, as a stereotype, no one will ever be able to pull our coat. So, first we have to go in the closet and find out where we are lacking, and what we need to replace that which we are lacking, [or] we never will be able to be successful. We can win with the ballot only when we make our people become politically mature.

Those whose philosophy is black nationalism are involved right now, and will become involved, with any group — green, blue, yellow, pink — that is set up with an organizational apparatus designed to get more of our people involved as registered voters. We're involved in that; we will cooperate with that. But at the same time we won't tell them to register as a Democrat or a Republican. Any Negro who registers as a Democrat or a Republican is a traitor to his own people.

Registering is all right. That only means "load your gun." Just because you load it doesn't mean you have to shoot it. You wait until you get a target and make certain that you're in a position to put that thing up next to the target, and then you pull the trigger. And just as you don't waste bullets at a target that's out of reach, you don't throw ballots just to be throwing ballots. Our people need to get registered, need to pile up political power, but they need to hold it in abeyance and throw it when they know that throwing it is going to get results. Don't just throw it because you've got it.

Question 11: (in writing — about concrete political plans)

Malcolm: This question: "Do you have any immediate concrete plans to take over politics and politicians in

black communities?" Yes, and when you've got concrete
plans, the best way to keep them concrete is keep them
to yourself.

Question 12: (in writing—about SNCC and the UN)

Malcolm: The other question written — "Excuse me,
but the Student Nonviolent Coordinating Committee ap-
pealed to the United Nations following the Birmingham
murders and picketed the UN demanding action for several days."

That's not how you get it—you don't get it picketing
the UN. In fact I have never seen anybody get anything
yet picketing. I haven't seen anything that was gotten
picketing. You get what you're going to get either one
way or the other. I might add to that. You don't get
anything on the agenda of the UN through picketing.

Plus, when the Student Nonviolent Coordinating Committee was picketing the UN based upon the murders
in Birmingham, it was still civil rights. They didn't have
enough sense to realize — excuse me for saying they
didn't have enough sense, but evidently they didn't—to
realize that as long as they took it from a civil rights
level the UN can't accept it. It must be human rights.
So the best thing for you to do, who are liberals, is to
go to the UN and get all of the books on human rights.

Do you know that the United States has never signed
the Covenant on Human Rights? It signed the Declaration of Human Rights, but it couldn't sign the Covenant
because in order to sign the Covenant, they'd have to
have it ratified by the Congress and the Senate. And
how're they going to get a covenant ratified by the Congress and the Senate on human rights when they can't
even get one through on civil rights? No! And Eleanor
Roosevelt, supposedly a liberal, was chairman of the
Commission on Human Rights. She knew all of this.
Why didn't ultra-liberal Eleanor tell these Negroes about
the UN section on human rights that would enable us
to get our problem before the world? No, that's why I
say I haven't met a white liberal. This gentleman over
here who thinks I'm going to discriminate [against]
him—[*Recognizes James Wechsler*]

Question 13: (about Rev. Bruce Klunder, who was killed by a bulldozer while demonstrating against school segregation in Cleveland)

Malcolm: I was in Cleveland last night, yesterday, in fact, when this thing took place — [*Wechsler speaks again*] Sir? I didn't put him under the bulldozer either. Uncle Sam put him under the bulldozer. The Supreme Court put him under the bulldozer. [*Wechsler again.*] His death still didn't desegregate the school system.

We're not going to stand up and applaud any contribution made by some individual white person when 22 million black people are dying every day. What he did — good, good, great. What he did — good. Hooray, hooray, hooray. Now Lumumba was murdered, Medgar Evers was murdered, Mack Parker was murdered, Emmett Till was murdered, my own father was murdered. You tell that stuff to somebody else. It's time that some white people started dying in this thing. If you'll forgive me, forgive me for saying so, but many more beside he are going when the wagon comes. Yes, sir?

Question 14: (about the religion of Islam and the partition of India)

Malcolm: If I understand you correctly, number one — you wanted to know why do we, black people, turn to Islam. The religion that many of our forefathers practiced before we were kidnapped and brought into this country by the American white man was the religion of Islam. This has been destroyed in textbooks of the American educational system to try and make it appear that we were nothing but animals or savages before we were brought here, to hide the criminal acts that they had to perpetuate upon us in order to bring us down to the level of animals that we're on today. But when you go back, you'll find that there were large Muslim empires that stretched all the way down into equatorial Africa, the Mali Empire, Guinea. All these places — their religion was Islam.

So here in America today when you find many of us who are accepting Islam as our religion we are only going back to the religion of our forefathers. Plus, we

believe that this is the religion that will do more to re-
form us of our weaknesses that we've become addicted
to here in Western society than any other religion. Sec-
ondly, we can see where Christianity has failed us 100
percent. They teach us to turn the other cheek, but they
don't turn it.

And concerning the partition of India and Pakistan —
I think that's what you meant — I'm not too familiar
with it other than the fact that I do know that for many
years the subcontinent of India was ruled by the British,
by the colonial powers from Europe. The strategy of
the colonial powers has always been to divide and conquer. As a rule you'll find that people in the East, in
the Orient, can pretty well live together. And I believe
when you find them fighting each other, you [should]
look for that man that's turning them one against the
other — divide and conquer. In fact, if Pakistan and
India had not been at each other's throats, so to speak,
for the past ten or so years, they probably could have
developed much faster and made more progress than
they have, and could do something more concrete toward helping us solve most of our problems. So these
divisions are dangerous.

Question 15: (about racial divisions in American society)

Malcolm: Well, we have. And you don't have to demand it. It's already divided on racial lines. Go to Harlem. All we're saying now is since we're already divided,
the least the government can do is let us control the
areas where we live. Let the white people control theirs,
let us control ours — that's all we're saying. If the white
man can control his, and actually what he's using to
control it is white nationalism, let us control ours with
black nationalism. You find white nationalism in the
white communities whether they are Catholic, whether
they are Jews, whether they are Protestant — they still
practice white nationalism. So all we're saying to our
people is to forget our religious differences. Forget all
the differences that have been artificially created by the
whites who have been over us, and try and work to-

gether in unity and harmony with the philosophy of black nationalism, which only means that we should control our own economy, our own politics, and our own society. Nothing is wrong with that.

And then, after we control our society, we'll work with any segment of the white community towards building a better civilization. But we think that they should control theirs and we should control ours. Don't let us try and mix with each other because every time that mixture takes place we always find the black man low man on the totem pole—*low* man on the totem pole. If he's not low man, he's no man at all. Yes, ma'am?

Question 16: (about the possibilities of support from Africa)

Malcolm: You'll find that here today in 1964 there are enough independent nations in the UN from Africa and Asia who have become politically mature and also have enough independence to do what is necessary to see that some results are gotten from any plea, bona fide plea, that's made on the part of our people. It was the control that the United States had in the UN that enabled them to get Lumumba murdered and have his murder covered up. But here's one things people are beginning to see. As soon as the United States gets through with a stooge, she drops him. She dropped Tshombe; when she couldn't use Tshombe anymore, she dropped him. When she couldn't use the two brothers over in Saigon—what's their names?—Diem and Nhu, she dropped them. When she couldn't use Syngman Rhee anymore, she dropped him. When she couldn't use Menderes anymore, she dropped him. Well, you see, this pattern is being studied by these other Uncle Toms. And they're beginning to see that if they keep on going, they're going to get dropped too. Yes, ma'am?

Question 17: (about the common interest of old age pensioners and black people)

Malcolm: I don't see how you can compare their situation with the plight of 22 million African-Americans. Our people were outright slaves—outright slaves. We pulled plows like horses. We were bought and sold from one plantation to another like you sell chickens or like you sell a bag of potatoes. I read in one book where George Washington exchanged a black man for a keg of molasses. Why, that black man could have been my grandfather. You know what I think of old George Washington. You can't compare someone on old age assistance with the plight of black people in this country. No comparison whatsoever. And what they can do is not comparable to what we can do — not those old folks. Yes, sir — way in the back.

Question 18: (about why the audience should stand in honor of Rev. Klunder)

Malcolm: Let's rise in the honor of Lumumba, let's rise in the honor of Medgar Evers, let's rise in the honor — No, look; good, what the man did is good. But the day is out when you'll find black people who are going to stand up and applaud the contribution of whites at this late date.

One hundred million Africans were uprooted from the African continent — where are they today? One hundred million Africans were uprooted, 100 million Africans, according to the book *Anti-Slavery*, by Professor Dwight Lowell Dumond — excuse me for raising my voice — were uprooted from the continent of Africa. At the end of slavery you didn't have 25 million Africans in the Western Hemisphere. What happened to those 75 million? Their bodies are at the bottom of the ocean, or their blood and their bones have fertilized the soil of this country. Why, don't you ever think I would use my energy applauding the sacrifice of an individual white man. No, that sacrifice is too late.

Question 19: (in writing — about black nationalism, separatism, integration and assimilation)

Malcolm: "A pamphlet, *Freedom Now*, is on sale in the back" — good plug — "and it contains the statement, 'All separatists are nationalists, but not all nationalists are separatists.'" I don't know anything about that. "What is your view on this? Can one be a black nationalist even though not interested in a separate independent black nation? Similarly, is every integrationist necessarily an assimilationist?"

Well, as I said earlier, the black people I know don't want to be integrationists, nor do they want to be separationists — they want to be human beings. Some of them choose integration, thinking that this method will bring them respect as a human being, and others choose separation, thinking that that method or tactic will bring them respect as a human being. But they've had so much trouble attaining their objectives that they've gotten their methods mixed up with their objectives. And now, instead of calling themselves human beings, they're calling themselves integrationists and separationists, and they don't have either one — no. So I don't know about the integrationists and the assimilationists and the separationists, but I do know about the segregationists — that's the Americans. Yes, sir?

Question 20: (about Malcolm's attitude to Robert F. Williams)

Malcolm: Well, Robert Williams was exiled to Cuba for advocating guns for Negroes. He made some mistakes in carrying out his program, which left the door open that allowed the FBI to make him appear to be the criminal that he actually is not. When someone in front of you makes a mistake, you should learn and benefit from those mistakes.

The black man in this country is within his constitutional rights to have a rifle. The white man is, too. The Constitution gives you the right to have a rifle or a shotgun. You shouldn't go out shooting people with it; you shouldn't become involved in acts of aggression that you initiate. But, in this country where we have a government, a law enforcement agency at the federal, local, and state level — in areas where those agencies show that they are unable or unwilling to defend Negroes, Negroes should defend themselves. That's all — should defend themselves. And he's within his lawful right. This doesn't mean that he should use arms to initiate acts of aggression. But if it costs me my life in the morning I will tell

you tonight that the time has come for the black man
to die fighting. If he's going to die, die fighting. I have
a rifle; I've shown my wife how to work it. And if anybody puts his foot on my step, he's dead. Whether I'm
home or not, he's dead.

This doesn't mean that we want to live in a society
like this. But when you're living in a society of criminals and the law fails to do its duty, what must one do?
Continue to turn the other cheek? Medgar Evers turned
his.   Those four little girls, who were bombed in a
church, turned theirs.   Negroes have done nothing but
seen each other turn the other cheek. This generation
won't do it, won't do it any longer. May I just say this,
sir? America is faced with a situation where in every Negro community in this country, the racial animosity that
is developing and the disillusionment in the minds of
Negroes toward white society is such that these communities, these ghettos, these slums that we live in, will eventually develop into the same type of Casbah situation
that you have in Algeria and these other countries—
where you won't be able to set your foot in that neighborhood, unless you've got a guide to show you the
way. This is true.

And what else should we do? How can we continue
to live in a community that's turned into a police state?
Where the police are not there to protect us but are there
only to protect the property of the merchant who doesn't
even live in our community, who has his store there and
his house somewhere else. They're there to protect his
property. And as Negroes over the years see this, we
also see that they don't protect us: in fact, sometimes we
need protection against *them*.

This doesn't mean that the police are always wrong—
I'm saying this too. In New York, where Negroes are
concerned, so-called Negroes, it has been my experience
in traveling from coast to coast to notice that in Harlem the police officer, at least in the past three years up
to a short while ago, exercised more care in dealing
with incidents that could explode into a racial situation
than is used by police officers in most of the large cities

of the North. In 1960, '61, '62, along in there, the police department here did use more caution in incidents
that were outright involving race. But the recent statement by the police commissioner, this man, this Irishman
Murphy, is very dangerous, because those commission-
ers who preceded him exercised more intelligence in statements that they made, and they were very careful never
to make a statement that would inflame the white officer
against the black community. But Murphy is making
statements that seem deliberately designed to make the
average cop on the beat think that he can bust any Negro up 'side his head and not be reprimanded for it.
This is dangerous because today when you put a club
in the direction of a Negro's head, he's going to do his
best to get that club, whether you've got a uniform or
not.

Question 21: (a general attack on Malcolm, followed
by a complaint that the speaker wants to make a statement rather than ask a question. Malcolm: "You can
comment right here, this is a meeting." After the speaker
denounces Malcolm further, some members of the audience begin to protest. Malcolm: "Let him have his say —
go ahead, Doctor." The speaker goes ahead.)

Malcolm: I'll take just two minutes to comment on
what you've said. You notice you kept using the expression "talk back" or "have their say." Now you know how
our people have felt for 400 years. And your attitude
right now is the type of attitude that makes Uncle Sam
a hated country. You reflect the collective attitudes of
the American whites.

There are some — he [*pointing to the chairman*] doesn't
reflect the collective attitude. He reflects the unique attitude — he's quiet, he's listening, he's taking it all in, he's
analyzing it. And when he stands up to speak, he's
going to speak in a much more intelligent manner than
you and will win more friends than you. Now I might
say this right here — in saying this about him, I'm not
saying this to jive him or pat him on the back. You
know me, I *think* you know me, better than that. If I
say positive things about him, I mean it. He will prob-

ably get some of you saved, but you will get most of you killed.

I just want to say one more comment on his remark about me being bloodthirsty. I'm not bloodthirsty. I'm one of 22 million black people in this country who's tired of being the victim of hypocrisy by a country that supposedly practices democracy. Any black man—you had your say, please be quiet—any black man who will stand up and tell you exactly how he feels is doing you a favor because most of them don't tell you how they feel.

I want to thank the Militant Labor Forum for the invitation to speak here this evening. I think, as I said earlier, the paper is one of the best that I've read. We always encourage those who live in Harlem to buy it when we see it up there, or wherever else we may see it. It's a very good paper. I hope they continue to have success, make progress. They can probably straighten out a lot of white people. Let us straighten out the black people. That's all I'm saying.

[Chairman turns over collection.]

And I want to thank you for the collection that was taken up — of $160.84 — which will go to further the awakening of our people in this country and helping you solve your problem. Thank you.

3 THE FOUNDING RALLY OF THE OAAU

Five days after the Militant Labor Forum talk, Malcolm X flew to the Mideast, where he first made his hajj to Mecca and then went on a tour of several African countries. Although he had expected to be gone only three weeks, the tour proved so valuable that he did not return until May 21.

This was not Malcolm's first visit to the Mideast and Africa. As he reported in the Autobiography, *he had been there briefly in 1959 as Muhammad's emissary. But the impact on him this time, when he had already begun to liberate himself from the bind of Muhammad's dogmas, was altogether different, in terms of his views both on race and politics. The fullest account of this trip and its effects on him appears in the* Autobiography.

Some commentators have criticized Malcolm for "wasting time" by this trip and his later, longer, trip to Africa and the Mideast; he should, they contend, have stayed at home and devoted all his energies to organizing Afro-Americans. Such criticism overlooks the fact that it was in Africa, among people mentioned in this speech whom

33

*he felt he could trust, that he found ideas and sugges-
tions which strengthened, deepened, matured and concret-
ized his revolutionary and internationalist convictions.
Without the African experience, Malcolm's growth surely
would have been less rapid and the development of revolutionary consciousness among Afro-Americans probably would have been slower. "Travel broadens your
scope," he said many times; in this particular case the
travel of one man helped to broaden the scope of millions.*

*When Malcolm was in Ghana in May, he decided
that in addition to the Muslim Mosque, Inc., another—
nonreligious—organization was needed. In fact, he and
Afro-Americans living in Ghana founded the first chapter of the new organization before he left that country.
As soon as he landed in New York, he got busy gather-
ing the forces for the new movement he thought was
needed to lead the struggle for "freedom by any means
necessary": the Organization of Afro-American Unity.
The first public rally of the OAAU (it was not a membership meeting) was held at the Audubon Ballroom
in New York on June 28, 1964. Malcolm gave two
speeches there, printed here for the first time.*

*In the first he read the "Statement of Basic Aims and
Objectives of the Organization of Afro-American Unity,"
a document which had been drawn up not by him but
by a committee of the new organization. Altering or
skipping a few words here and there as he read it, he
interspersed his own inimitable comments as he went
along. (The document itself is printed as an appendix
in* The Last Year of Malcolm X.*) In the second speech
he discussed and explained the structure and perspec-
tives of the new organization; a few errors of fact were
made in his remarks on voting and registration pro-
cedures, for which he used notes prepared by someone
else.*

*These speeches are notable for the themes to which
they addressed themselves — themes that were to be
raised as demands and programs and fought for in*

*black communities throughout the country in the years
following Malcolm's death. The speeches are also typical
of Malcolm's best talks to black audiences — in their
directness, simplicity, seriousness, humor, and unsur-
passed ability to educate and inspire.*

Salaam Alaikum, Mr. Moderator, our distinguished
guests, brothers and sisters, our friends and our enemies,
everybody who's here.

As many of you know, last March when it was announced that I was no longer in the Black Muslim movement, it was pointed out that it was my intention to
work among the 22 million non-Muslim Afro-Americans
and to try and form some type of organization, or create a situation where the young people — our young
people, the students and others — could study the problems of our people for a period of time and then come
up with a new analysis and give us some new ideas and
some new suggestions as to how to approach a problem
that too many other people have been playing around
with for too long. And that we would have some kind
of meeting and determine at a later date whether to form
a black nationalist party or a black nationalist army.

There have been many of our people across the country from all walks of life who have taken it upon themselves to try and pool their ideas and to come up with
some kind of solution to the problem that confronts all
of our people. And tonight we are here to try and get
an understanding of what it is they've come up with.

Also, recently when I was blessed to make a religious
pilgrimage to the holy city of Mecca where I met many
people from all over the world, plus spent many weeks
in Africa trying to broaden my own scope and get more
of an open mind to look at the problem as it actually
is, one of the things that I realized, and I realized this
even before going over there, was that our African brothers have gained their independence faster than you and
I here in America have. They've also gained recogni-

tion and respect as human beings much faster than you
and I.

Just ten years ago on the African continent, our people
were colonized. They were suffering all forms of colonization, oppression, exploitation, degradation, humiliation, discrimination, and every other kind of -ation. And
in a short time, they have gained more independence,
more recognition, more respect as human beings than
you and I have. And you and I live in a country which
is supposed to be the citadel of education, freedom, justice, democracy, and all of those other pretty-sounding
words.

So it was our intention to try and find out what it was
our African brothers were doing to get results, so that
you and I could study what they had done and perhaps
gain from that study or benefit from their experiences.
And my traveling over there was designed to help to
find out how.

One of the first things that the independent African
nations did was to form an organization called the Organization of African Unity. This organization consists
of all independent African states who have reached the
agreement to submerge all differences and combine their
efforts toward eliminating from the continent of Africa
colonialism and all vestiges of oppression and exploitation being suffered by African people. Those who formed
the organization of African states have differences. They
represent probably every segment, every type of thinking. You have some leaders that are considered Uncle
Toms, some leaders who are considered very militant.
But even the militant African leaders were able to sit
down at the same table with African leaders whom they
considered to be Toms, or Tshombes, or that type of
character. They forgot their differences for the sole purpose of bringing benefits to the whole. And whenever
you find people who can't forget their differences, then
they're more interested in their personal aims and objectives than they are in the conditions of the whole.

Well, the African leaders showed their maturity by
doing what the American white man said couldn't be

done. Because if you recall when it was mentioned that these African states were going to meet in Addis Ababa, all of the Western press began to spread the propaganda that they didn't have enough in common to come together and to sit down together. Why, they had Nkrumah there, one of the most militant of the African leaders, and they had Adoula from the Congo. They had Nyerere there, they had Ben Bella there, they had Nasser there, they had Sékou Toure, they had Obote; they had Kenyatta—I guess Kenyatta was there, I can't remember whether Kenya was independent at that time, but I think he was there. Everyone was there and despite their differences, they were able to sit down and form what was known as the Organization of African Unity, which has formed a coalition and is working in conjunction with each other to fight a common enemy.

Once we saw what they were able to do, we determined to try and do the same thing here in America among Afro-Americans who have been divided by our enemies. So we have formed an organization known as the Organization of Afro-American Unity which has the same aim and objective—to fight whoever gets in our way, to bring about the complete independence of people of African descent here in the Western Hemisphere, and first here in the United States, and bring about the freedom of these people by any means necessary.

That's our motto. We want freedom by any means necessary. We want justice by any means necessary. We want equality by any means necessary. We don't feel that in 1964, living in a country that is supposedly based upon freedom, and supposedly the leader of the free world, we don't think that we should have to sit around and wait for some segregationist congressmen and senators and a President from Texas in Washington, D. C., to make up their minds that our people are due now some degree of civil rights. No, we want it now or we don't think anybody should have it.

The purpose of our organization is to start right here in Harlem, which has the largest concentration of people of African descent that exists anywhere on this earth.

There are more Africans in Harlem than exist in any
city on the African continent. Because that's what you
and I are — Africans. You catch any white man off guard
in here right now, you catch him off guard and ask
him what he is, he doesn't say he's an American. He
either tells you he's Irish, or he's Italian, or he's German, if you catch him off guard and he doesn't know
what you're up to. And even though he was born here,
he'll tell you he's Italian. Well, if he's Italian, you and
I are African — even though we were born here.

So we start in New York City first. We start in Harlem — and by Harlem we mean Bedford-Stuyvesant, any
place in this area where you and I live, that's Harlem —
with the intention of spreading throughout the state,
and from the state throughout the country, and from
the country throughout the Western Hemisphere. Because when we say Afro-American, we include everyone in the Western Hemisphere of African descent. South
America is America. Central America is America. South
America has many people in it of African descent. And
everyone in South America of African descent is an Afro-
American. Everyone in the Caribbean, whether it's the
West Indies or Cuba or Mexico, if they have African
blood, they are Afro-Americans. If they're in Canada
and they have African blood, they're Afro-Americans.
If they're in Alaska, though they might call themselves
Eskimos, if they have African blood, they're Afro-Amer-
icans.

So the purpose of the Organization of Afro-American
Unity is to unite everyone in the Western Hemisphere
of African descent into one united force. And then, once
we are united among ourselves in the Western Hemisphere, we will unite with our brothers on the motherland, on the continent of Africa. So to get right with it,
I would like to read you the "Basic Aims and Objectives
of the Organization of Afro-American Unity," started
here in New York, June, 1964.

"The Organization of Afro-American Unity, organized
and structured by a cross section of the Afro-American

people living in the United States of America, has been patterned after the letter and spirit of the Organization of African Unity which was established at Addis Ababa, Ethiopia, in May of 1963.

"We, the members of the Organization of Afro-American Unity, gathered together in Harlem, New York:

"Convinced that it is the inalienable right of all our people to control our own destiny;

"Conscious of the fact that freedom, equality, justice and dignity are central objectives for the achievement of the legitimate aspirations of the people of African descent here in the Western Hemisphere, we will endeavor to build a bridge of understanding and create the basis for Afro-American unity;

"Conscious of our responsibility to harness the natural and human resources of our people for their total advancement in all spheres of human endeavor;

"Inspired by our common determination to promote understanding among our people and cooperation in all matters pertaining to their survival and advancement, we will support the aspirations of our people for brotherhood and solidarity in a larger unity transcending all organizational differences;

"Convinced that, in order to translate this determination into a dynamic force in the cause of human progress conditions of peace and security must be established and maintained;" — And by "conditions of peace and security," [we mean] we have to eliminate the barking of the police dogs, we have to eliminate the police clubs, we have to eliminate the water hoses, we have to eliminate all of these things that have become so characteristic of the American so-called dream. These have to be eliminated. Then we will be living in a condition of peace and security. We can never have peace and security as long as one black man in this country is being bitten by a police dog. No one in the country has peace and security.

"Dedicated to the unification of all people of African descent in this hemisphere and to the utilization of that

unity to bring into being the organizational structure
that will project the black people's contributions to the
world;

"Persuaded that the Charter of the United Nations,
the Universal Declaration of Human Rights, the Constitution of the United States and the Bill of Rights are
the principles in which we believe and that these docu-
ments if put into practice represent the essence of man-
kind's hopes and good intentions;

"Desirous that all Afro-American people and organizations should henceforth unite so that the welfare and
well-being of our people will be assured;

"We are resolved to reinforce the common bond of
purpose between our people by submerging all of our
differences and establishing a nonsectarian, constructive
program for human rights;

"We hereby present this charter.

"I — Establishment.

"The Organization of Afro-American Unity shall
include all people of African descent in the Western Hemisphere, as well as our brothers and sisters on the African
continent." Which means anyone of African descent, with
African blood, can become a member of the Organization of Afro-American Unity, and also any one of our
brothers and sisters from the African continent. Because
not only it is an organization of Afro-American unity
meaning that we are trying to unite our people in the
West, but it's an organization of Afro-American unity in
the sense that we want to unite all of our people who are
in North America, South America, and Central America
with our people on the African continent. We must unite
together in order to go forward together. Africa will not
go forward any faster than we will and we will not go
forward any faster than Africa will. We have one destiny and we've had one past.

In essence, what it is saying is instead of you and me
running around here seeking allies in our struggle for
freedom in the Irish neighborhood or the Jewish neighborhood or the Italian neighborhood, we need to seek
some allies among people who look something like we

do. It's time now for you and me to stop running away from the wolf right into the arms of the fox, looking for some kind of help. That's a drag.

"II — Self Defense.

"Since self-preservation is the first law of nature, we assert the Afro-American's right to self-defense.

"The Constitution of the United States of America clearly affirms the right of every American citizen to bear arms. And as Americans, we will not give up a single right guaranteed under the Constitution. The history of unpunished violence against our people clearly indicates that we must be prepared to defend ourselves or we will continue to be a defenseless people at the mercy of a ruthless and violent racist mob.

"We assert that in those areas where the government is either unable or unwilling to protect the lives and property of our people, that our people are within our rights to protect themselves by whatever means necessary." I repeat, because to me this is the most important thing you need to know. I already know it. "We assert that in those areas where the government is either unable or unwilling to protect the lives and property of our people, that our people are within our rights to protect themselves by whatever means necessary."

This is the thing you need to spread the word about among our people wherever you go. Never let them be brainwashed into thinking that whenever they take steps to see that they're in a position to defend themselves that they're being unlawful. The only time you're being unlawful is when you break the law. It's lawful to have something to defend yourself. Why, I heard President Johnson either today or yesterday, I guess it was today, talking about how quick this country would go to war to defend itself. Why, what kind of a fool do you look like, living in a country that will go to war at the drop of a hat to defend itself, and here you've got to stand up in the face of vicious police dogs and blue-eyed crackers waiting for somebody to tell you what to do to defend yourself!

Those days are over, they're gone, that's yesterday.

The time for you and me to allow ourselves to be brutalized nonviolently is *passé*. Be nonviolent only with those who are nonviolent to you. And when you can bring me a nonviolent racist, bring me a nonviolent segregationist, then I'll get nonviolent. But don't teach me to be nonviolent until you teach some of those crackers to be nonviolent. You've never seen a nonviolent cracker. It's hard for a racist to be nonviolent. It's hard for anyone intelligent to be nonviolent. Everything in the universe does something when you start playing with his life, except the American Negro. He lays down and says, "Beat me, daddy."

So it says here: "A man with a rifle or a club can only be stopped by a person who defends himself with a rifle or a club." That's equality. If you have a dog, I must have a dog. If you have a rifle, I must have a rifle. If you have a club, I must have a club. This is equality. If the United States government doesn't want you and me to get rifles, then take the rifles away from those racists. If they don't want you and me to use clubs, take the clubs away from the racists. If they don't want you and me to get violent, then stop the racists from being violent. Don't teach us nonviolence while those crackers are violent. Those days are over.

"Tactics based solely on morality can only succeed when you are dealing with people who are moral or a system that is moral. A man or system which oppresses a man because of his color is not moral. It is the duty of every Afro-American person and every Afro-American community throughout this country to protect its people against mass murderers, against bombers, against lynchers, against floggers, against brutalizers and against exploiters."

I might say right here that instead of the various black groups declaring war on each other, showing how militant they can be cracking each other's heads, let them go down South and crack some of those crackers' heads. Any group of people in this country that has a record of having been attacked by racists — and there's no record where they have ever given the signal to take the heads of some of those racists—why, they are insane giving the signal to take the heads of some of their ex-brothers. Or brother X's, I don't know how you put that.

"III — Education

"Education is an important element in the struggle for human rights. It is the means to help our children and our people rediscover their identity and thereby increase their self-respect. Education is our passport to the future, for tomorrow belongs only to the people who prepare for it today."

And I must point out right there, when I was in Africa I met no African who wasn't standing with open arms to embrace any Afro-American who returned to the African continent. But one of the things that all of them have said is that every one of our people in this country should take advantage of every type of educational opportunity available before you even think about talking about the future. If you're surrounded by schools, go to that school.

"Our children are being criminally shortchanged in the public school system of America. The Afro-American schools are the poorest-run schools in the city of New York. Principals and teachers fail to understand the nature of the problems with which they work and as a result they cannot do the job of teaching our children." They don't understand us, nor do they understand our problems; they don't. "The textbooks tell our children nothing about the great contributions of Afro-Americans to the growth and development of this country."

And they don't. When we send our children to school in this country they learn nothing about us other than that we used to be cotton pickers. Every little child going to school thinks his grandfather was a cotton picker. Why, your grandfather was Nat Turner; your grandfather was Toussaint L'Ouverture; your grandfather was Hannibal. Your grandfather was some of the greatest black people who walked on this earth. It was your grandfather's hands who forged civilization and it was your grandmother's hands who rocked the cradle of civilization. But the textbooks tell our children nothing

about the great contributions of Afro-Americans to the
growth and development of this country.

"The Board of Education's integration plan is expen-
sive and unworkable; and the organization of principals
and supervisors in New York City's school system has
refused to support the Board's plan to integrate the
schools, thus dooming it to failure before it even starts.

"The Board of Education of this city has said that
even with its plan there are 10 percent of the schools
in Harlem and the Bedford-Stuyvesant community in
Brooklyn that they cannot improve." So what are we to
do? "This means that the Organization of Afro-American
Unity must make the Afro-American community a more
potent force for educational self-improvement.

"A first step in the program to end the existing system
of racist education is to demand that the 10 percent of
the schools the Board of Education will not include in
its plan be turned over to and run by the Afro-American community itself." Since they say that they can't
improve these schools, why should you and I who live
in the community, let these fools continue to run and
produce this low standard of education? No, let them
turn those schools over to us. Since they say they can't
handle them, nor can they correct them, let us take a
whack at it.

What do we want? "We want Afro-American principals
to head these schools. We want Afro-American teachers
in these schools." Meaning we want black principals and
black teachers with some textbooks about black people.
"We want textbooks written by Afro-Americans that are
acceptable to our people before they can be used in these
schools.

"The Organization of Afro-American Unity will select
and recommend people to serve on local school boards
where school policy is made and passed on to the Board
of Education." And this is very important.

"Through these steps we will make the 10 percent of
the schools that we take over educational showplaces
that will attract the attention of people from all over the
nation." Instead of them being schools turning out pupils
whose academic diet is not complete, we can turn them

into examples of what we can do ourselves once given
an opportunity.

"If these proposals are not met, we will ask Afro-American parents to keep their children out of the present
inferior schools they attend. And when these schools in
our neighborhood are controlled by Afro-Americans,
we will then return our children to them.

"The Organization of Afro-American Unity recognizes
the tremendous importance of the complete involvement
of Afro-American parents in every phase of school life.
The Afro-American parent must be willing and able to
go into the schools and see that the job of educating our
children is done properly." This whole thing about putting all of the blame on the teacher is out the window.
The parent at home has just as much responsibility to
see that what's going on in that school is up to par as
the teacher in their schools. So it is our intention not
only to devise an education program for the children,
but one also for the parents to make them aware of
their responsibility where education is concerned in regard to their children.

"We call on all Afro-Americans around the nation to
be aware that the conditions that exist in the New York
City public school system are as deplorable in their
cities as they are here. We must unite our efforts and
spread our program of self-improvement through education to every Afro-American community in America.

"We must establish all over the country schools of our
own to train our own children to become scientists, to
become mathematicians. We must realize the need for
adult education and for job retraining programs that
will emphasize a changing society in which automation
plays the key role. We intend to use the tools of education to help raise our people to an unprecedented level
of excellence and self-respect through their own efforts.

"IV — Politics and Economics."

And the two are almost inseparable, because the politician is depending on some money; yes, that's what
he's depending on.

"Basically, there are two kinds of power that count in
America: economic power and political power, with so-

cial power being derived from those two. In order for
the Afro-Americans to control their destiny, they must
be able to control and affect the decisions which control
their destiny: economic, political, and social. This can
only be done through organization.

"The Organization of Afro-American Unity will organize the Afro-American community block by block to
make the community aware of its power and its potential; we will start immediately a voter registration drive
to make every unregistered voter in the Afro-American
community an independent voter."

We won't organize any black man to be a Democrat
or a Republican because both of them have sold us out.
Both of them have sold us out; both parties have sold
us out. Both parties are racist, and the Democratic Party
is more racist than the Republican Party. I can prove
it. All you've got to do is name everybody who's running the government in Washington, D. C., right now.
He's a Democrat and he's from either Georgia, Alabama,
Texas, Mississippi, Florida, South Carolina, North Carolina, from one of those cracker states. And they've got
more power than any white man in the North has. In
fact, the President is from a cracker state. What's he talking about? Texas is a cracker state, in fact, they'll hang
you quicker in Texas than they will in Mississippi. Don't
you ever think that just because a cracker becomes president he ceases being a cracker. He was a cracker before
he became president and he's a cracker while he's president. I'm going to tell it like it is. I hope you can take
it like it is.

"We propose to support and organize political clubs,
to run independent candidates for office, and to support
any Afro-American already in office who answers to
and is responsible to the Afro-American community."
We don't support any black man who is controlled by
the white power structure. We will start not only a voter
registration drive, but a voter education drive to let our
people have an understanding of the science of politics
so they will be able to see what part the politician plays
in the scheme of things; so they will be able to under-

stand when the politician is doing his job and when he is not doing his job. And any time the politician is not doing his job, we remove him whether he's white, black, green, blue, yellow or whatever other color they might invent.

"The economic exploitation in the Afro-American community is the most vicious form practiced on any people in America." In fact, it is the most vicious practiced on any people on this earth. No one is exploited economically as thoroughly as you and I, because in most countries where people are exploited they know it. You and I are in this country being exploited and sometimes we don't know it. "Twice as much rent is paid for rat-infested, roach-crawling, rotting tenements."

This is true. It costs us more to live in Harlem than it costs them to live on Park Avenue. Do you know that the rent is higher on Park Avenue in Harlem than it is on Park Avenue downtown? And in Harlem you have everything else in that apartment with you — roaches, rats, cats, dogs, and some other outsiders — disguised as landlords. "The Afro-American pays more for food, pays more for clothing, pays more for insurance than anybody else." And we do. It costs you and me more for insurance than it does the white man in the Bronx or somewhere else. It costs you and me more for food than it does them. It costs you and me more to live in America than it does anybody else, and yet we make the greatest contribution.

You tell me what kind of country this is. Why should we do the dirtiest jobs for the lowest pay? Why should we do the hardest work for the lowest pay? Why should we pay the most money for the worst kind of food and the most money for the worst kind of place to live in? I'm telling you we do it because we live in one of the rottenest countries that has ever existed on this earth. It's the system that is rotten; we have a rotten system. It's a system of exploitation, a political and economic system of exploitation, of outright humiliation, degradation, discrimination — all of the negative things that you can run into, you have run into under this system that disguises itself as a democracy, disguises itself as a democracy. And the things that they practice against you and me are worse than some of the things that they practiced in Germany against the Jews. Worse than some of the things that the Jews ran into. And you run around here getting ready to get drafted and go someplace and defend it. Someone needs to crack you up 'side your head.

"The Organization of Afro-American Unity will wage an unrelenting struggle against these evils in our community. There shall be organizers to work with our people to solve these problems, and start a housing self-improvement program." Instead of waiting for the white man to come and straighten out our neighborhood, we'll straighten it out ourselves. This is where you make your mistake. An outsider can't clean up your house as well as you can. An outsider can't take care of your children as well as you can. An outsider can't look after your needs as well as you can. And an outsider can't understand your problems as well as you can. Yet you're looking for an outsider to do it. *We* will do it or it will never get done.

"We propose to support rent strikes." Yes, not little, small rent strikes in one block. We'll make Harlem a rent strike. We'll get every black man in this city; the Organization of Afro-American Unity won't stop until there's not a black man in the city not on strike. Nobody will pay any rent. The whole city will come to a halt. And they can't put all of us in jail because they've already got the jails full of us.

Concerning our social needs — I hope I'm not frightening anyone. I should stop right here and tell you if you're the type of person who frights, who gets scared, you should never come around us. Because we'll scare you to death. And you don't have far to go because you're half dead already. Economically you're dead — dead broke. Just got paid yesterday and dead broke right now.

"V — Social.

"This organization is responsible only to the Afro-

American people and the Afro-American community."
This organization is not responsible to anybody but us.
We don't have to ask the man downtown can we demonstrate. We don't have to ask the man downtown what
tactics we can use to demonstrate our resentment against
his criminal abuse. We don't have to ask his consent; we
don't have to ask his endorsement; we don't have to ask
his permission. Anytime we know that an unjust condition exists and it is illegal and unjust, we will strike at
it by any means necessary. And strike also at whatever
and whoever gets in the way.

"This organization is responsible only to the Afro-
American people and community and will function only
with their support, both financially and numerically. We
believe that our communities must be the sources of their
own strength politically, economically, intellectually, and
culturally in the struggle for human rights and human
dignity.

"The community must reinforce its moral responsibility to rid itself of the effects of years of exploitation, neglect, and apathy, and wage an unrelenting struggle
against police brutality." Yes. There are some good policemen and some bad policemen. Usually we get the bad
ones. With all the police in Harlem, there is too much
crime, too much drug addiction, too much alcoholism,
too much prostitution, too much gambling.

So it makes us suspicious about the motives of Commissioner Murphy when he sends all these policemen
up here. We begin to think that they are just his errand
boys, whose job it is to pick up the graft and take it
back downtown to Murphy. Anytime there's a police
commissioner who finds it necessary to increase the
strength numerically of the policemen in Harlem and,
at the same time, we don't see any sign of a decrease in
crime, why, I think we're justified in suspecting his motives. He can't be sending them up here to fight crime,
because crime is on the increase. The more cops we
have, the more crime we have. We begin to think that
they bring some of the crime with them.

So our purpose is to organize the community so that

we ourselves — since the police can't eliminate the drug
traffic, we have to eliminate it. Since the police can't
eliminate organized gambling, we have to eliminate it.
Since the police can't eliminate organized prostitution
and all of these evils that are destroying the moral fiber
of our community, it is up to you and me to eliminate
these evils ourselves. But in many instances, when you
unite in this country or in this city to fight organized
crime, you'll find yourselves fighting the police department itself because they are involved in the organized
crime. Wherever you have organized crime, that type
of crime cannot exist other than with the consent of the
police, the knowledge of the police and the cooperation
of the police.

You'll agree that you can't run a number in your
neighborhood without the police knowing it. A prostitute can't turn a trick on the block without the police
knowing it. A man can't push drugs anywhere along
the avenue without the police knowing it. And they pay
the police off so that they will not get arrested. I know
what I'm talking about — I used to be out there. And I
know you can't hustle out there without police setting
you up. You have to pay them off.

The police are all right. I say there's some good ones
and some bad ones. But they usually send the bad ones
to Harlem. Since these bad police have come to Harlem and have not decreased the high rate of crime, I tell
you brothers and sisters it is time for you and me to
organize and eliminate these evils ourselves, or we'll be
out of the world backwards before we even know where
the world was.

Drug addiction turns your little sister into a prostitute
before she gets into her teens; makes a criminal out of
your little brother before he gets in his teens — drug addiction and alcoholism. And if you and I aren't men
enough to get at the root of these things, then we don't
even have the right to walk around here complaining
about it in any form whatsoever. The police will not
eliminate it. "Our community must reinforce its moral
responsibility to rid itself of the effects of years of ex-

ploitation, neglect, and apathy, and wage an unrelenting struggle against police brutality."

Where this police brutality also comes in — the new law that they just passed, the no-knock law, the stop-and-frisk law, that's an anti-Negro law. That's a law that was passed and signed by Rockefeller. Rockefeller with his old smile, always he has a greasy smile on his face and he's shaking hands with Negroes, like he's the Negro's pappy or granddaddy or great-uncle. Yet when it comes to passing a law that is worse than any law that they had in Nazi Germany, why, Rockefeller couldn't wait till he got his signature on it. And the only thing this law is designed to do is make legal what they've been doing all the time.

They've passed a law that gives them the right to knock down your door without even knocking on it. Knock it down and come on in and bust your head and frame you up under the disguise that they suspect you of something. Why, brothers, they didn't have laws that bad in Nazi Germany. And it was passed for you and me, it's an anti-Negro law, because you've got an anti-Negro governor sitting up there in Albany — I started to say Albany, Georgia — in Albany, New York. Not too much difference. Not too much difference between Albany, New York, and Albany, Georgia. And there's not too much difference between the government that's in Albany, New York, and the government in Albany, Georgia.

" The Afro-American community must accept the responsibility for regaining our people who have lost their place in society. We must declare an all-out war on organized crime in our community; a vice that is controlled by policemen who accept bribes and graft must be exposed. We must establish a clinic, whereby one can get aid and cure for drug addiction."

This is absolutely necessary. When a person is a drug addict, he's not the criminal; he's a victim of the criminal. The criminal is the man downtown who brings this drug into the country. Negroes can't bring drugs into this country. You don't have any boats. You don't

have any airplanes. You don't have any diplomatic im-
munity. It is not you who is responsible for bringing in
drugs. You're just a little tool that is used by the man
downtown. The man that controls the drug traffic sits
in city hall or he sits in the state house. Big shots who
are respected, who function in high circles — those are
the ones who control these things. And you and I will
never strike at the root of it until we strike at the man
downtown.

"We must create meaningful, creative, useful activities
for those who were led astray down the avenues of vice.

"The people of the Afro-American community must
be prepared to help each other in all ways possible; we
must establish a place where unwed mothers can get
help and advice." This is a problem, this is one of the
worst problems in our . . .

[*A short passage is lost here as the tape is turned.*]

"We must set up a guardian system that will help our
youth who get into trouble." Too many of our children
get into trouble accidentally. And once they get into
trouble, because they have no one to look out for them,
they're put in some of these homes where others who
are experienced at getting in trouble are. And immediately it's a bad influence on them and they never have
a chance to straighten out their lives. Too many of our
children have their entire lives destroyed in this manner.
It is up to you and me right now to form the type of
organizations wherein we can look out for the needs of
all of these young people who get into trouble, especially
those who get into trouble for the first time, so that we
can do something to steer them back on the right path
before they go too far astray.

"And we must provide constructive activities for our
own children. We must set a good example for our children and must teach them to always be ready to accept
the responsibilities that are necessary for building good
communities and nations. We must teach them that their
greatest responsibilities are to themselves, to their fam-
ilies and to their communities.

"The Organization of Afro-American Unity believes

that the Afro-American community must endeavor to do the major part of all charity work from within the community. Charity, however, does not mean that to which we are legally entitled in the form of government benefits. The Afro-American veteran must be made aware of all the benefits due to him and the procedure for obtaining them."

Many of our people have sacrificed their lives on the battlefront for this country. There are many government benefits that our people don't even know about. Many of them are qualified to receive aid in all forms, but they don't even know it. But *we* know this, so it is our duty, those of us who know it, to set up a system wherein our people who are not informed of what is coming to them, we inform them, we let them know how they can lay claim to everything that they've got coming to them from this government. And I mean you've got much coming to you. " The veterans must be encouraged to go into business together, using GI loans." and all other items that we have access to or have available to us.

"Afro-Americans must unite and work together. We must take pride in the Afro-American community, for it is our home and it is our power," the base of our power.

"What we do here in regaining our self-respect, our manhood, our dignity and freedom helps all people everywhere who are also fighting against oppression."

Lastly, concerning culture and the cultural aspect of the Organization of Afro-American Unity.

"'A race of people is like an individual man; until it uses its own talent, takes pride in its own history, expresses its own culture, affirms its own selfhood, it can never fulfill itself.'"

"Our history and our culture were completely destroyed when we were forcibly brought to America in chains. And now it is important for us to know that our history did not begin with slavery. We came from Africa, a great continent, wherein live a proud and varied people, a land which is the new world and was the cradle of civilization. Our culture and our history are as old as man himself and yet we know almost nothing about it."

This is no accident. It is no accident that such a high state of culture existed in Africa and you and I know nothing about it. Why, the man knew that as long as you and I thought we were somebody, he could never treat us like we were nobody. So he had to invent a system that would strip us of everything about us that we could use to prove we were somebody. And once he had stripped us of all human chacteristics — stripped us of our language, stripped us of our history, stripped us of all cultural knowledge, and brought us down to the level of an animal — he then began to treat us like an animal, selling us from one plantation to another, selling us from one owner to another, breeding us like you breed cattle.

Why, brothers and sisters, when you wake up and find out what this man here has done to you and me, you won't even wait for somebody to give the word. I'm not saying all of them are bad. There might be some good ones. But we don't have time to look for them. Not nowadays.

"We must recapture our heritage and our identity if we are ever to liberate ourselves from the bonds of white supremacy. We must launch a cultural revolution to unbrainwash an entire people." A cultural revolution. Why, brothers, that's a crazy revolution. When you tell this black man in America who he is, where he came from, what he had when he was there, he'll look around and ask himself, "Well, what happened to it, who took it away from us and how did they do it?" Why, brothers, you'll have some action just like that. When you let the black man in America know where he once was and what he once had, why, he only needs to look at himself now to realize something criminal was done to him to bring him down to the low condition that he's in today.

Once he realizes what was done, how it was done, where it was done, when it was done, and who did it, that knowledge in itself will usher in your action program. And it will be by any means necessary. A man doesn't know how to act until he realizes what he's acting against. And you don't realize what you're acting against until you realize what they did to you. Too many of you don't know what they did to you, and this is what makes you so quick to want to forget and forgive. No, brothers, when you see what has happened to you, you will never forget and you'll never forgive. And, as I say, all of them might not be guilty. But most of them are. Most of them are.

"Our cultural revolution must be the means of bringing us closer to our African brothers and sisters. It must begin in the community and be based on community participation. Afro-Americans will be free to create only when they can depend on the Afro-American community for support, and Afro-American artists must realize that they depend on the Afro-American community for inspiration."

Our artists—we have artists who are geniuses; they don't have to act the Stepin Fetchit role. But as long as they're looking for white support instead of black support, they've got to act like the old white supporter wants them to. When you and I begin to support the black artists, then the black artists can play that black role. As long as the black artist has to sing and dance to please the white man, he'll be a clown, he'll be clowning, just another clown. But when he can sing and dance to please black men, he sings a different song and he dances a different step. When we get together, we've got a step all our own. We have a step that nobody can do but us, because we have a reason for doing it that nobody can understand but us.

"We must work toward the establishment of a cultural center in Harlem, which will include people of all ages and will conduct workshops in all of the arts, such as film, creative writing, painting, theater, music, and the entire spectrum of Afro-American history.

"This cultural revolution will be the journey to our rediscovery of ourselves. History is a people's memory, and without a memory man is demoted to the level of the lower animals." When you have no knowledge of your history, you're just another animal; in fact, you're a Negro; something that's nothing. The only black man on earth who is called a Negro is one who has no knowledge of his history. The only black man on earth who is called a Negro is one who doesn't know where he came from. That's the one in America. They don't call Africans Negroes.

Why, I had a white man tell me the other day, "He's not a Negro." Here the man was black as night, and the white man told me, "He's not a Negro, he's an African." I said, "Well, listen to him." I knew he wasn't, but I wanted to pull old whitey out, you know. But it shows you that they know this. You are Negro because you don't know who you are, you don't know what you are, you don't know where you are, and you don't know how you got here. But as soon as you wake up and find out the positive answer to all these things, you cease being a Negro. You become somebody.

"Armed with the knowledge of our past, we can with confidence charter a course for our future. Culture is an indispensable weapon in the freedom struggle. We must take hold of it and forge the future with the past."

And to quote a passage from *Then We Heard the Thunder* by John Killens, it says: *"'He was a dedicated patriot: Dignity was his country, Manhood was his government, and Freedom was his land.'" Old John Killens.

This is our aim. It's rough, we have to smooth it up some. But we're not trying to put something together that's smooth. We don't care how rough it is. We don't care how tough it is. We don't care how backward it may sound. In essence it only means we want one thing. We declare our right on this earth to be a man, to be a human being, to be respected as a human being, to be given the rights of a human being in this society, on this earth, in this day, which we intend to bring into existence by any means necessary.

I'm sorry I took so long. But before we go farther to tell you how you can join this organization, what your

---

*Omitted here is the introductory line of the quotation in Killens' book: "When the battle is won, let history be able to say to each one of us:"

duties and responsibilities are, I want to turn you back into the hands of our master of ceremonies, Brother Les Edmonds.

[*A collection is taken. Malcolm resumes:*]

One of the first steps we are going to become involved in as an Organization of Afro-American Unity will be to work with every leader and other organization in this country interested in a program designed to bring your and my problem before the United Nations. This is our first point of business. We feel that the problem of the black man in this country is beyond the ability of Uncle Sam to solve it. It's beyond the ability of the United States government to solve it. The government itself isn't capable of even hearing our problem, much less solving it. It's not morally equipped to solve it.

So we must take it out of the hands of the United States government. And the only way we can do this is by internationalizing it and taking advantage of the United Nations Declaration of Human Rights, the United Nations Charter on Human Rights, and on that ground bring it into the UN before a world body wherein we can indict Uncle Sam for the continued criminal injustices that our people experience in this government.

To do this, we will have to work with many organizations and many people. We've already gotten promises of support from many different organizations in this country and from many different leaders in this country and from many different independent nations in Africa, Asia, and Latin America. So this is our first objective and all we need is your support. Can we get your support for this project?

For the past four weeks since my return from Africa, several persons from all walks of life in the Afro-American community have been meeting together, pooling knowledge and ideas and suggestions, forming a sort of a brain trust, for the purpose of getting a cross section of thinking, hopes, aspirations, likes and dislikes, to see what kind of organization we could put together that would in some way or other get the grass-roots support, and what type of support it would need in order to be independent enough to take the type of action necessary to get results.

No organization that is financed by white support can ever be independent enough to fight the power structure with the type of tactics necessary to get real results. The only way we can fight the power structure, and it's the power structure that we're fighting — we're not even fighting the Southern segregationists, we're fighting a system that is run in Washington, D. C. That's the seat of the system that we're fighting. And in order to fight it, we have to be independent of it. And the only way we can be independent of it is to be independent of all support from the white community. It's a battle that we have to wage ourselves.

Now, if white people want to help, they can help. But they can't join. They can help in the white community, but they can't join. We accept their help. They can form the White Friends of the Organization of Afro-American Unity and work in the white community on white people and change their attitude toward us. They don't ever need to come among us and change our attitude. We've had enough of them working around us trying to change our attitude. That's what got us all messed up.

So we don't question their sincerity, we don't question their motives, we don't question their integrity. We just encourage them to use it somewhere else — in the white community. If they can use all of this sincerity in the white community to make the white community act better toward us, then we'll say, " Those are good white folks." But they don't have to come around us, smiling at us and showing us all their teeth like white Uncle Toms, to try and make themselves acceptable to us. The White Friends of the Organization of Afro-American Unity, let them work in the white community.

The only way that this organization can be independent is if it is financed by you. It must be financed by you. Last week I told you that it would cost a dollar to join it. We sat down and thought about it all week long and said that charging you a dollar to join it would not make it an organization. We have set a membership joining fee, if that's the way you express it, at $2.00. It costs more than that, I think, to join the NAACP.

By the way, you know I attended the NAACP convention Friday in Washington, D. C., which was very enlightening. And I found the people very friendly. They've got the same kind of ideas you have. They act a little different, but they've got the same kind of ideas, because they're catching the same hell we're catching. I didn't find any hostility at that convention at all. In fact, I sat and listened to them go through their business and learned a lot from it. And one of the things I learned is they only charge, I think, $2.50 a year for membership, and that's it. Well, this is one of the reasons that they have problems. Because any time you have an organization that costs $2.50 a year to belong to, it means that that organization has to turn in another direction for funds. And this is what castrates it. Because as soon as the white liberals begin to support it, they tell it what to do and what not to do.

This is why Garvey was able to be more militant. Garvey didn't ask them for help. He asked our people for help. And this is what we're going to do. We're going to try and follow his books.

So we're going to have a $2.00 joining fee and ask every member to contribute a dollar a week. Now, the NAACP gets $2.50 a year, that's it. And it can't ever go anywhere like that because it's always got to be putting on some kind of drive for help and will always get its help from the wrong source. And then when they get that help, they'll have to end up condemning all the enemies of their enemy in order to get some more help. No, we condemn our enemies, not the enemies of our enemies. We condemn our enemies.

So what we are going to ask you to do is, if you want to become a member of the Organization of Afro-American Unity, it will cost you $2.00. We are going to ask you to pay a dues of a dollar a week. We will have an accountant, a bookkeeping system, which will keep the members up-to-date as to what has come in, what has been spent, and for what. Because the secret to success

in any kind of business venture — and anything that you
do that you mean business, you'd better do in a busi-
nesslike way — the secret to your success is keeping good
records, good organized records.

Since today will be the first time that we are opening
the books for membership, our next meeting will be next
Sunday here. And we will then have a membership. And
we'll be able to announce at that time the officers of the
Organization of Afro-American Unity. I'll tell you the
top officer is the chairman, and that's the office I'm
holding. I'm taking the responsibility of the chairman,
which means I'm responsible for any mistakes that take
place; anything that goes wrong, any failures, you can
rest them right upon my shoulders. So next week the
officers will be announced.

And this week I wanted to tell you the departments in
this organization that, when you take out your membership, you can apply to work in. We have the department
of education. The department of political action. For all
of you who are interested in political action, we will
have a department set up by brothers and sisters who
are students of political science, whose function it will
be to give us a breakdown of the community of New
York City. First, how many assemblymen there are and
how many of those assemblymen are black, how many
congressmen there are and how many of those congressmen are black. In fact, let me just read something real
quick and I'll show you why it's so necessary. Just to
give you an example.

There are 270,000 eligible voters in the twenty-first
senatorial district. The twenty-first senatorial district is
broken down into the eleventh, seventh, and thirteenth
assembly districts. Each assembly district contains 90,-
000 eligible voters. In the eleventh assembly district,
only 29,000 out of 90,000 eligible voters exercise their
voting rights. In the seventh assembly district, only 36,-
000 out of the 90,000 eligible voters vote. Now, in a
white assembly district with 90,000 eligible voters, 65,-
000 exercise their voting rights, showing you that in the
white assembly districts more whites vote than blacks

vote in the black assembly districts. There's a reason for this. It is because our people aren't politically aware of what we can get by becoming politically active.

So what we have to have is a program of political education to show them what they can get if they take political action that's intelligently directed. Less than 25 percent of the eligible voters in Harlem vote in the primary election. Therefore, they have not the right to place the candidate of their choice in office, as only those who were in the primary can run in the general election. The following number of signatures are required to place a candidate to vote in the primaries: for assemblyman it must be 350 signatures; state senator, 750; countywide judgeship, 1,000; borough president, 2,250; mayor, 7,500. People registered with the Republican or Democratic parties do not have to vote with their party.

There are fifty-eight senators in the New York state legislature. Four are from Manhattan; one is black. In the New York state assembly, there are 150 assemblymen. I think three are black; maybe more than that. According to calculation, if the Negro were proportionately represented in the state senate and state assembly, we would have several representatives in the state senate and several in the state assembly. There are 435 members in the United States House of Representatives. According to the census, there are 22 million Afro-Americans in the United States. If they were represented proportionately in this body, there would be 30 to 40 members of our race sitting in that body. How many are there? Five. There are 100 senators in the United States Senate. Hawaii, with a population of only 600 thousand, has two senators representing it. The black man, with a population of in excess of 20 million, is not represented in the Senate at all. Worse than this, many of the congressmen and representatives in the Congress of the United States come from states where black people are killed if they attempt to exercise the right to vote.

What you and I want to do in this political department is have our brothers and sisters who are experts in the science of politics acquaint our people in our com-

munity with what we should have, and who should be
doing it, and how we can go about getting what we
should have. This will be their job and we want you
to play this role so we can get some action without having to wait on Lyndon B. Johnson, Lyndon B. Texas
Johnson.

Also, our economics department. We have an economics department. For any of you who are interested in
business or a program that will bring about a situation
where the black man in Harlem can gain control over
his own economy and develop business expansion for
our people in this community so we can create some
employment opportunities for our people in this community, we will have this department.

We will also have a speakers bureau because many
of our people want to speak, want to be speakers, they
want to preach, they want to tell somebody what they
know, they want to let off some steam. We will have a
department that will train young men and young women
how to go forth with our philosophy and our program
and project it throughout the country; not only throughout this city but throughout the country.

We will have a youth group. The youth group will be
designed to work with youth. Not only will it consist of
youth, but it will also consist of adults. But it will be
designed to work out a program for the youth in this
country, one in which the youth can play an active part.

We also are going to have our own newspaper. You
need a newspaper. We believe in the power of the press.
A newspaper is not a difficult thing to run. A newspaper
is very simple if you have the right motives. In fact,
anything is simple if you have the right motives. The
Muhammad Speaks newspaper, I and another person
started it myself in my basement. And I've never gone
past the eighth grade. Those of you who have gone to
all these colleges and studied all kinds of journalism, yellow and black journalism, all you have to do is contribute some of your journalistic talent to our newspaper
department along with our research department, and
we can turn out a newspaper that will feed our people

with so much information that we can bring about a real live revolution right here before you know it.

We will also have a cultural department. The task or duty of the cultural department will be to do research into the culture, into the ancient and current culture of our people, the cultural contributions and achievements of our people. And also all of the entertainment groups that exist on the African continent that can come here and ours who are here that can go there. Set up some kind of cultural program that will really emphasize the dormant talent of black people.

When I was in Ghana I was speaking with, I think his name is Nana Nketsia, I think he's the minister of culture or he's head of the culture institute. I went to his house, he had a—he had a nice, beautiful place; I started to say he had a sharp pad. He had a fine place in Accra. He had gone to Oxford, and one of the things that he said impressed me no end. He said that as an African his concept of freedom is a situation or a condition in which he, as an African, feels completely free to give vent to his own likes and dislikes and thereby develop his own African personality. Not a condition in which he is copying some European cultural pattern or some European cultural standard, but an atmosphere of complete freedom where he has the right, the leeway, to bring out of himself all of that dormant, hidden talent that has been there for so long.

And in that atmosphere, brothers and sisters, you'd be surprised what will come out of the bosom of this black man. I've seen it happen. I've seen black musicians when they'd be jamming at a jam session with white musicians—a whole lot of difference. The white musician can jam if he's got some sheet music in front of him. He can jam on something that he's heard jammed before. If he's heard it, then he can duplicate it or he can imitate it or he can read it. But that black musician, he picks up his horn and starts blowing some sounds that he never thought of before. He improvises, he creates, it comes from within. It's his soul, it's that soul music. It's the only area on the American scene where the black man has been free to create. And he has mastered it. He has shown that he can come up with something that nobody ever thought of on his horn.

Well, likewise he can do the same thing if given intellectual independence. He can come up with a new philosophy. He can come up with a philosophy that nobody has heard of yet. He can invent a society, a social system, an economic system, a political system, that is different from anything that exists or has ever existed anywhere on this earth. He will improvise; he'll bring it from within himself. And this is what you and I want.

You and I want to create an organization that will give us so much power we can sit down and do as we please. Once we can sit down and think as we please, speak as we please, and do as we please, we will show people what pleases us. And what pleases us won't always please them. So you've got to get some power before you can be yourself. Do you understand that? You've got to get some power before you can be yourself. Once you get power and you be yourself, why, you're gone, you've got it and gone. You create a new society and make some heaven right here on this earth.

And we're going to start right here tonight when we open up our membership books into the Organization of Afro-American Unity. I'm going to buy the first memberships myself—one for me, my wife, Attillah, Qubilah, these are my daughters, Ilyasah, and something else I expect to get either this week or next week. As I told you before, if it's a boy I'm going to name him Lumumba, the greatest black man who ever walked the African continent.

He didn't fear anybody. He had those people so scared they had to kill him. They couldn't buy him, they couldn't frighten him, they couldn't reach him. Why, he told the king of Belgium, "Man, you may let us free, you may have given us our independence, but we can never forget these scars." The greatest speech — you should take that speech and tack it up over your door.

This is what Lumumba said: "You aren't giving us anything. Why, can you take back these scars that you put
on our bodies? Can you give us back the limbs that
you cut off while you were here?" No, you should never
forget what that man did to you. And you bear the
scars of the same kind of colonization and oppression
not on your body, but in your brain, in your heart, in
your soul, right now.

So, if it's a boy, Lumumba. If it's a girl, Lumumbah.

[*Malcolm introduces several people from the platform
and from the audience, then continues:*]

If I passed over some of the rest of you, it's because
my eyes aren't too good, my glasses aren't too good.
But everybody here are people who are from the street
who want some kind of action. We hope that we will be
able to give you all the action you need. And more than
likely we'll be able to give you more than you want. We
just hope that you stay with us.

Our meeting will be next Sunday night right here. We
want you to bring all of your friends and we'll be able
to go forward. Up until now, these meetings have been
sponsored by the Muslim Mosque, Inc. They've been
sponsored and paid for by the Muslim Mosque, Inc.
Beginning next Sunday, they will be sponsored and
paid for by the Organization of Afro-American Unity.

I don't know if I'm right in saying this, but for a
period of time, let's you and me not be too hard on
other Afro-American leaders. Because you would be surprised how many of them have expressed sympathy and
support in our efforts to bring this situation confronting our people before the United Nations. You'd be surprised how many of them, some of the last ones you
would expect, they're coming around. So let's give them
a little time to straighten up. If they straighten up, good.
They're our brothers and we're responsible for our
brothers. But if they don't straighten up, then that's another point.

And one thing that we are going to do, we're going to
dispatch a wire, a telegram that is, in the name of the

Organization of Afro-American Unity to Martin Luther
King in St. Augustine, Florida, and to Jim Forman in
Mississippi, worded in essence to tell them that if the
federal government doesn't come to their aid, call on
us. And we will take the responsibility of slipping some
brothers into that area who know what to do by any
means necessary.

I can tell you right now that my purpose is not to become involved in a fight with Black Muslims, who are
my brothers still. I do everything I can to avoid that
because there's no benefit in it. It actually makes our
enemy happy. But I do believe that the time has come
for you and me to take the responsibility of forming
whatever nucleus or defense group is necessary in places
like Mississippi. Why, they shouldn't have to call on the
federal government—that's a drag. No, when you and
I know that our people are the victims of brutality, and
all times the police in those states are the ones who are
responsible, then it is incumbent upon you and me, if
we are men, if we are to be respected and recognized, it
is our duty . . .

[*A passage is lost here through a defect in the tape.*]

Johnson knew that when he sent [Allen] Dulles down
there. Johnson has found this out. You don't disappear.
How are you going to disappear? Why, this man can
find a missing person in China. They send the CIA all
the way to China and find somebody. They send the
FBI anywhere and find somebody. But they can't find
them whenever the criminal is white and the victim is
black, then they can't find them.

Let's don't wait on any more FBI to look for criminals who are shooting and brutalizing our people. Let's
you and me find them. And I say that it's easy to do
it. One of the best-organized groups of black people in
America was the Black Muslims. They've got all the
machinery, don't think they haven't; and the experience
where they know how to ease out in broad daylight or
in dark and do whatever is necessary by any means
necessary. They know how to do that. Well, I don't
blame anybody for being taught how to do that. You're

living in a society where you're the constant victim of brutality. You must know how to strike back.

So instead of them and us wasting our shots, I should say our time and energy, on each other, what we need to do is band together and go to Mississippi. That's my closing message to Elijah Muhammad: If he is the leader of the Muslims and the leader of our people, then lead us against our enemies, don't lead us against each other.

I thank you for your patience here tonight, and we want each and every one of you to put your name on the roll of the Organization of Afro-American Unity. The reason we have to rely upon you to let the public know where we are is because the press doesn't help us; they never announce in advance that we're going to have a meeting. So you have to spread the word over the grapevine. Thank you. Salaam Alaikum.

The founding meeting of the Organization of Afro-American Unity, June 28, 1964.

4 HARLEM AND THE POLITICAL MACHINES

The following excerpts, printed for the first time, comprise almost half of a radio program broadcast by Station WLIB in New York on July 4, 1964. Participants in the program, called "The Editors Speak," were George W. Goodman, WLIB public affairs director; George S. Schuyler of the New York Courier; *Allan Morrison of* Ebony *and* Jet; *and Malcolm X.*

In his remarks here Malcolm called Adam Clayton Powell an "independent" politician, but it is necessary to observe that he immediately added, "Whether he uses his independence for good or bad is another question." He said the OAAU was not committed to supporting Powell in the coming election, and as a matter of fact it did not endorse him that year. Whatever else Malcolm meant at that time by "independent," it did not necessarily imply political support of Powell.

Also noteworthy is Malcolm's concept of his relation to the OAAU: "the OAAU is not me . . . we take matters collectively." If the OAAU's weakness was that it was too much a "one-man" operation, as some asserted later, it was certainly not because that was what Malcolm had in mind.

George W. Goodman: You are going to build an organization. Your organization, at the moment, is centered in New York City.

Malcolm X: Yes, Harlem.

Goodman: What are you going to do about these problems here? How do you plan to implement the activities of your organization in the solution of those?

Malcolm: First, I go for what Nkrumah says, when he says "Seek ye first the political kingdom" and so forth. Our people have not only a voter registration drive on here for Harlem; we also have a voter education drive, to educate the masses of our people into the science of politics, and what politics is supposed to produce for us, what the politician is supposed to do for us. Then we will have a better understanding of whether or not these politicians are producing or whether they are fulfilling their promises. Once we can get our people actively engaged in politics, not just following the political machines, but involved in politics with an understanding of what they are doing, why they are doing it, what they should be getting out of it, and their responsibility in the political arena, we feel that we will then be in a better position to bring pressure on the politicians who now exploit our people and perpetuate conditions of poverty and slums and vice and other forms of crime that exist in the Harlem community. Where education is concerned we feel that our people should be given a complete understanding of how we can keep the level of education of the schools in our community up; how we can make quality education exist right here in Harlem without having to ship our children someplace else; how we can bring pressure to bear on the power structure downtown to keep the level of the schools in Harlem up, or build larger schools, or whatever the situation may be.

Goodman: May I ask just one practical question?

Malcolm: Yes.

Goodman: Are you going to go out to register people as Democrats, as Republicans, or what? Are you going to fight the party machines?

Malcolm: We are going to encourage our people to register as independent voters. First become registered.

George S. Schuyler: How can you do this?

Malcolm: You can register as an independent. We feel that there are more unregistered Negroes in Harlem than there are registered Negroes in both parties. So that any grass-roots operation — and we already have the thing set up where we can register them house by house, we can organize them house by house, block by block, and get the active participation of the people who up to this time have displayed some form of lethargy. Actually it isn't lethargy, it's suspicion. They don't believe that any leader or any organization will produce for them the things that they need. So they withdraw from active involvement. But we think we can get them involved.

Schuyler: Well, that may not be so dumb. You just think they're dumb because they're not following you.

Malcolm: No, I told you that they aren't refraining from becoming involved through lethargy; this is what I said. The masses of black people know what they are doing when they don't become actively involved. But if anybody can bring up a program or produce a program for them which they feel will get them some meaningful results, I believe that you will find that our people at the mass level will become as actively involved in politics as upper-class Negroes are now involved.

Goodman: What you are saying, Minister Malcolm X, is that the political life and activity in the Negro community is controlled by the Negro middle class. Do you propose to change the power basis from the middle class to the working and low-income people?

Malcolm: The Negro middle class doesn't even control

it. They are used by the man downtown to control the
Negro uptown.

Goodman: They run the political organizations.

Malcolm: Yes, but we intend to try and get a mass
involvement, mass participation, and we believe that
we can do this by carrying on an education program,
where politics is concerned, among the masses to make
them see what those who now control the political picture are doing to them. We believe that through politics
and through the politician you can actually change the
deplorable school situation in Harlem.

Schuyler: Won't you have to do that through a political organization? You just can't have people indiscriminately —

Malcolm: The Organization of Afro-American Unity
will be just as political as any organization in Harlem;
but we will be more politically active for the good of the
people and the good of the community than most other —

Schuyler: How is it going to function differently from
Tammany Hall, the Republicans, and the other organizations?

Malcolm: Well, let us say that Tammany Hall func-
tions for the good of the white power structure by and
large, and we will set up a black Tammany Hall that's
for the good of Harlem. . . .

Roy Wilkins, I think, once said that if he could add
an additional million Negroes to the rolls of registered
voters throughout the country, what a difference it would
make. We think that we can get almost every Negro in
New York City registered if we give him the right program. We believe that our people will become actively
involved in anything that they have confidence in, if
they feel that it is for their good.

Schuyler: Now what is it that hasn't been done before?

Malcolm: I think that in the past we have been mostly
exploited, politically, economically, and every other way
that you can think of. You know the only real independent Negro politician in this country is Adam Clayton
Powell. Whether he uses his independence for good or
bad is another question and another subject. But the
only real independent Negro politician in this country

is Adam Clayton Powell. He's the only one who's ever been able to buck the political machines and still stay in office. This is primarily because the people here in Harlem are more prone toward bucking the power structure than is often the case in other parts of the country. So once Powell realizes that the people also are aware of the fact that he is independent, then he is also more conscious of his duty to the people and what he must produce for them in order to stay in office.

Allan Morrison: Seeing that you've brought in the name of one individual, prominent, nationally-known Negro politician, Representative Adam Clayton Powell, I am curious now as to whether your organization has committed itself to supporting him in the forthcoming election.

Malcolm: It hasn't committed itself to supporting anyone. It has committed itself to supporting that which is good for black people. Between now and the time of the election it will sit down and analyze the entire political situation and come up with an answer that we feel will be good for the whole.

Morrison: You know, Mr. Schuyler, one of our panelists here, is an opponent of Mr. Powell in the coming election, a candidate for the Conservative Party. I am sure that he doesn't share your sentiments about Congressman Powell at all. But I was wondering whether he stands a chance of endorsement by the OAAU?

Malcolm: Well, you'd have to ask the OAAU. The OAAU is not me. I am the chairman, but we take matters collectively.

Goodman: I would like to get in just a question for a minute to Mr. Schuyler. Do you plan to oppose this organization, Mr. Schuyler, in your field?

Schuyler: I hadn't anticipated it. But I would like to know what about Mr. Dawson? Mr. Dawson in Chicago seems to have tremendous power there. He's been reelected year after year.

Malcolm: Mr. Dawson gets his power from the machine. Dawson's power, the base of his power, is the machine.

Schuyler: So does Powell's machine, doesn't it?

Malcolm: His power is from the white machine itself. Whereas Powell's power is from people out there in the street. Powell bucks the machine.

Schuyler: You've certainly got to cooperate with the powers-that-be if you're going to operate politically.

Malcolm: We find that most Negroes in that collaboration end up being collaborated right on out of the pie.

5 THE SECOND RALLY OF THE OAAU

*The second rally of the OAAU was held at the Audubon
Ballroom on July 5, 1964, shortly after the adoption of
the Civil Rights Act of 1964, and shortly before the out-
break of the so-called Harlem "riot," which Malcolm X
later was to call a police pogrom*

It is helpful to understand that the OAAU rallies were
not membership meetings. They were educational events,
open to the public and the press, where Malcolm and
others discussed and explained current and general
problems and tried to persuade the audience to join the
OAAU. When time allowed, they included a question
and discussion period. The July 5 discussion period was
supposed to last five or ten minutes, but actually continued for at least forty.

An examination of the entire June 28 tape supports
Malcolm's contention that he had never named Gloria
Richardson of Cambridge, Maryland, Rev. Albert Cleage
of Detroit, and Jesse Gray of Harlem as members of an
OAAU "brain trust." In fact, he never mentioned their
names at all, although the chairman, Les Edmonds, had

reported the receipt of greetings from Miss Richardson and Rev. Cleage, among others.

Malcolm's July 5 remarks about demonstrations— "If whatever you are demonstrating for isn't worth dying for, don't demonstrate"— are more representative of the militant-sounding rationalizations used by the Black Muslims to abstain from demonstrations than they are of his subsequent views. At OAAU and other meetings later in the year, he abandoned this all-or-nothing approach and supported demonstrations for more limited objectives, although he never did become an advocate of demonstrations-just-to-be-doing-something.

The reference to Christine Keeler is to a figure in a sex scandal involving a British cabinet member; those to Wagner, Donovan, and Gross are to the then-mayor and two officials of the Board of Education of New York City; and the one to the Congo is to the very start of U.S. intervention in the Congolese civil war, which was to assume much bigger proportions later in the year.

Those questions on the tape which could not be heard clearly or fully are summarized. The following excerpts are printed for the first time.

Salaam Alaikum. Brothers and sisters, I think we have a very nice audience here this evening taking into consideration that this is a holiday weekend when normally you and I would be out on the beach rubbing elbows with those other elbows. So I want to thank those of you who have taken off from the beach and those many other places and taken the time to come out here this evening so that we can try and get a better understanding of what we must do and therefore what we are going to do.

Before starting out— I don't know if anybody is here from the *New York Journal American*. Is anybody here from the *New York Journal American*? The reason I would like to know, and if anybody comes in from the *New York Journal American* please let me know, is be-

cause last Wednesday they had a headline in here saying that Malcolm X plans to take over, which to me is
a deliberately concocted blue-eyed lie.

This person, who professes to be named Martin Arun-
del, whatever kind of name that is, on the front page of
this paper went on to explain how I had named last
Sunday Gloria Richardson, Albert Cleage, and Jesse
Gray and several others as part of a brain trust responsible for setting up the OAAU. I doubt that any of you
who are sitting here heard me mention those names last
Sunday. But here's a man who reported it just like he
heard it.

And this is one of the reasons why you have such
bad racial problems on this earth today. You tell lies
about us. And we get to believing that you just might
be what we had been told you are. At least all the evidence leads in that direction. So this particular paper,
the *New York Journal American*, filled its front page on
Wednesday with nothing but lies allegedly giving an
account of what took place here last Sunday.

And I very much doubt that this person was here.

Also it mentioned that I attacked the civil rights leaders, which I didn't do. I didn't attack anybody but the
man who has been brutal to us. And it isn't the civil
rights leaders who have been brutal. They've been the
victims of brutality. They have been loving you all while
you all have been hating them. So I didn't attack them.
I probably questioned their intelligence in letting you
beat them without fighting back. But I don't think that
we attacked them. In fact, we sent them a telegram, we
sent Martin Luther King a telegram, letting him know
that if he needed any help, we'd come on the run. Does
that sound like we're attacking civil rights leaders? No,
we're telling them that they need some help and we'll
help them. But not nonviolently.

You'll excuse me for opening up the meeting on that
note, but it is very trying on one's patience to have to
listen to white people day in and day out say that we
bar them from our meetings, or that we don't like them,
or that our attitude is sort of bitter. And then when you

let them into your meeting, they prove that you should
have kept them out of it in the first place. I guess bad
white people put you good ones on the spot, don't they?

On Thursday of this week, or I think it was Friday,
there was a great hullaballoo made over the recent passage of the civil rights bill. On the front pages of all the
newspapers the day after it was supposedly signed so
that it was in effect, they had pictures of little black boys
sitting in barbershop chairs letting white barbers cut
their hair. And this was hailed as a great victory. Pick
up on that.

In 1964, when oppressed people all over this earth
are fighting for their place in the sun, the Negro in
America is supposed to stand up and cheer because he
can sit down and let a white man mess up his head.

At the same time that so much hullaballoo was being
made over the passage of the civil rights bill, if you
read closly between the lines, a little black boy in Georgia was found hung on a tree. A 1964 June lynching.
Nothing was said in the paper, no hullaballoo was
made over that. But here's a little fourteen-year-old black
boy in Georgia lynched, and to keep you and me from
knowing what was taking place, they showed another
picture of a little black boy letting a white man cut his
hair.

This is the trickery that you and I are faced with
every day in this society. They on the one hand try and
show us how much progress we're making. But if we
look through all of that propaganda we find that our
people are still being hung, they're still disappearing,
and no one is finding them, or no one is finding their
murderers.

And at the same time also that so much hullaballoo
was being made over this new civil rights legislation,
a bill went into effect known as the no-knock law or
stop-and-frisk law, which was an anti-Negro law. They
make one law that's outright against Negroes and make
it appear that it is for our people, while at the same
time they pass another bill that's supposedly designed
to give us some kind of equal rights. You know, sooner

or later you and I are going to wake up and be fed
up, and there's going to be trouble. There's got to be
trouble.

While they were making so much hullaballoo again
over the passage of these new civil rights bills or legislation, they could not deny the fact that all these new
laws are aimed at the South. None of them are aimed
at the North. Nothing in this legislation is designed to
straighten out the situation that you and I are confronted
with here in New York City. There's nothing in the bill
that will stop job discrimination in New York, that will
stop housing discrimination in New York, that will stop
educational discrimination in New York. There's nothing in the bill that will stop the police from exercising
police state tactics in New York. There's nothing in the
bill that touches on your and my problem here in New
York City. Everything in the bill deals with our people
in the South.

We are interested in our people in the South. But we
have to question whether or not this bill, these laws,
will help our people in the South when ten years ago
the Supreme Court came up with a law called the deseg-
regated school law, or something to that effect, which
hasn't been enforced yet. And you and I would be children, we would be boys, we would be mental midgets,
if we let the white man even make us *think* that some
new laws were going to be enforced in Mississippi, Alabama, Georgia, and Texas while the Supreme Court
law has not yet been enforced in New York City. You'd
be out of your mind to even look happy. And you'd be
way out of your mind to make them think that you're
happy.

No, when you and I know that these political tricks
are being pulled, if you and I don't let it be known that
we know it, why, they'll keep on with their skullduggery
and their trickery, and they will think that the problem
is being solved when actually they're only compounding
it and making it worse. If they can't enforce laws that
are laid down by the Supreme Court, which is the land's
highest court, do you think that they can enforce some

new laws in Mississippi, Alabama, and Georgia? And
if they can't enforce these new laws, then why do they
pretend? Why come up with the bill? What is all this
hullaballoo for? It's nothing but twentieth-century trickery, some more of the same old legislative trickery that
you and I and our mothers and fathers have been hand-
ed for the past fifty, sixty, or one hundred years.

Prior to one hundred years ago, they didn't need
tricks. They had chains. And they needed the chains because you and I hadn't yet been brainwashed thoroughly enough to submit to their brutal acts of violence sub-
missively. Prior to a hundred years ago, you had men
like Nat Turner, that Brother Benjamin was talking
about, and others, Toussaint L'Ouverture. None of them
would submit to slavery. They'd fight back by any
means necessary. And it was only after the spirit of the
black man was completely broken and his desire to be
a man was completely destroyed, then they had to use
different tricks. They just took the physical chains from
his ankles and put them on his mind.

And from then on, the type of slavery that you and
I have been experiencing, we've been kept in it, year
in and year out, by a change of tricks. Never do they
change our condition or the slavery. They only change
the tricks. This is done from the White House right on
down to the plantation boss in Alabama and Mississippi.
Right on down from the White House you are tricked,
right on down to the plantation boss in Mississippi and
Alabama. There is no difference between the plantation
boss in Mississippi and the plantation boss in Washington, D. C. Both of them are plantation bosses. What
you experience in this country is one huge plantation
system, the only difference now being that the President
is the plantation boss.

And he's got a whole lot of well-known celebrity-style
Negroes to act as overseers, to keep us in check. When
we begin to get too bad, they jump in and say, now,
let's be responsible, or let's be intelligent, or let's don't
go too fast, let's slow down. But it's still a slave system.

It's only brought about in a more modern way, a more up-to-date form of slavery.

Proof of which, of the people who just got off the boat yesterday in this country, from the various so-called Iron Curtain countries, which are supposedly an enemy to this country, and no civil rights legislation is needed to bring them into the mainstream of the American way of life, then you and I should just stop and ask ourselves, why is it needed for us? They're actually slapping you and me in the face when they pass a civil rights bill. It's not an honor; it's a slap in the face. They're telling you that you don't have it, and at the same time they're telling you that they have to legislate before you can get it. Which in essence means they're telling you that since you don't have it and yet you're born here, there must be something about you that makes you different from everybody else who's born here; something about you that actually, though you have the right of birth in this land, you're still not qualified under their particular system to be recognized as a citizen.

Yet the Germans, that they used to fight just a few years ago, can come here and get what you can't get. The Russians, whom they're supposedly fighting right now, can come here and get what you can't get without legislation; don't need legislation. The Polish don't need legislation. Nobody needs it but you. Why? — you should stop and ask yourself why. And when you find out why, then you'll change the direction you've been going in, and you'll change also the methods that you've been using trying to get in that direction. . . .

We've got to seek some new methods, a reappraisal of the situation, some new methods for attacking it or solving it, and a new direction, and new allies. We need allies who are going to help us achieve a victory, not allies who are going to tell us to be nonviolent. If a white man wants to be your ally, what does he think of John Brown? You know what John Brown did? He went to war. He was a white man who went to war against white people to help free slaves. He wasn't non-

violent. White people call John Brown a nut. Go read
the history, go read what all of them say about John
Brown. They're trying to make it look like he was a
nut, a fanatic. They made a movie on it, I saw a movie
on the screen one night. Why, I would be afraid to get
near John Brown if I go by what other white folks say
about him.

But they depict him in this image because he was willing
to shed blood to free the slaves. And any white man who
is ready and willing to shed blood for your freedom —
in the sight of other whites, he's nuts. As long as he
wants to come up with some nonviolent action, they
go for that, if he's liberal, a nonviolent liberal, a love-
everybody liberal. But when it comes time for making
the same kind of contribution for your and my freedom
that was necessary for them to make for their own freedom, they back out of the situation. So, when you want
to know good white folks in history where black people
are concerned, go read the history of John Brown. That
was what I call a white liberal. But those other kind,
they are questionable.

So if we need white allies in this country, we don't
need those kind who compromise. We don't need those
kind who encourage us to be polite, responsible, you
know. We don't need those kind who give us that kind
of advice. We don't need those kind who tell us how
to be patient. No, if we want some white allies, we need
the kind that John Brown was, or we don't need you.

And the only way to get those kind is to turn in a
new direction.

Now this may anger some of you who've been involved
in protests and demonstrations and other things. Maybe you don't realize it, but I think most of us here do.
The days of demonstrations of protest are over. They're
outdated. All that does is put you in jail. You've got
to pay money to get out. And you still haven't solved
the problem. Go and find out how much money has
been paid by demonstrators for court, for legal fees,
bail bonds, during the past five or six years. And then

find out what has been gained from it and you'll see that we're in the red. We're broke.

Plus, a protest demonstration is an act that is a reaction to what someone else has done. And as long as you're involved in it, you're in someone else's bag. You're reacting to what they've done. And all they have to do to keep you on their string is keep situations developing to keep you reacting, to keep you so busy you never have a chance to sit down and figure out a constructive program of your own that will enable you and me to make the progress that is our due.

An example. A demonstration is all right if it's going to get results. Oh, yes. But a demonstration just to demonstrate is a waste of time. If someone touches one of us and we want to go where the guilty person is, we all go together. But we don't go just to walk around the block with a sign. No, we go to get the one who harmed us — that's a demonstration, that's what's known as positive action. You don't go and march around someone to let him know you don't like what he did. Why, you can stay home and let him know you don't like what he did. If he's got any sense, he knows that you shouldn't like what he did. No, that stuff is outdated.

The kind of a demonstration you and I want and need is one that gets positive results. Not a one-day demonstration, but a demonstration until the end, the end of whatever we're demonstrating against. That's a demonstration. Don't say that you don't like what I did and you're going to come out and walk in front of my house for an hour. No, you're wasting your time. I'll sit down and go to sleep until your hour is up. If we're going to demonstrate, it should be a demonstration based upon no-holds-barred.

[*Voice from audience: "The sooner the better."*]

I know, the sooner the better. But, then again, *not* the sooner the better. Because whenever black people are independent enough to come up with the type of demonstration that is necessary to get results, there's going to be bloodshed. Because in a real demonstration, the white man's going to resist—yes, he is. So if you're not for some all-out action, you shouldn't get involved in any kind of action. This is all I'm saying. If whatever you are demonstrating for isn't worth dying for, don't demonstrate. Your demonstration is in vain.

And when I say whenever it isn't worth dying for, I don't mean one-way dying. Dying must be reciprocal, mutual; some dying on both sides. If it's not worth that, stay home.

Please just try and understand. Anything that involves a large number of people can always get out of hand, which means it can always bring death to you. Any kind of demonstration that you're in can bring death to you, especially when you're in a society that believes in brutality. So when you get involved in a large demonstration, you can die. But you should not be willing to die alone. So, if you should not be willing to die alone, it also involves taking the lives of others. And if it is not worth your taking the lives of others, then don't demonstrate. This is what you must understand. Any cause that can cost you your life must be the type of cause in which you yourself are willing to take life.

If it can cost you your life and you aren't willing to take life, do you realize what you are doing to yourself? Why, you're walking into a lion's den with your hands tied. If it is not worth dying for, get out of it. If it can cost you your life and, at the same time, you aren't psychologically prepared to take life, stay out of it. Get out of it. All you'll do is get in the way. You'll make someone have to do something unnecessarily. You'll go and get yourself killed, and your brother will have to go and take the head that took your head. And your head isn't even worth it.

So all of these off-the-wall, excuse the expression, activities that we've been maneuvered into during the past ten years—we don't want that. The Organization of Afro-American Unity was formed by brothers and sisters, black, brown, red, and yellow, from the Afro-American community for the purpose of trying to devise some kind of positive program that would enable us to take positive steps toward getting some positive results. And one of the first aims of this organization is to internationalize your and my problem. . . .

Even in these demonstrations that brought about token integration, the only reason he gave up some tokens was because the world was watching him. He didn't do it because your protest changed him. This is what you've got to understand. Why, you can protest against this man all day long. It's no change of heart that makes him back up. He looks across the water and sees the world looking at him. And he changes only to the degree that you have reached world opinion. If you have reached world opinion, he changes. But you don't change his opinion. No. And if you don't understand that, then you need to crawl back in the cotton patch. Because that's where you belong. You don't belong out here on the world stage.

And if it took world pressure to bring us the gains, whatever gains we've made, then what should we do today? Continue to look to Washington, D. C.? No, look to the world. Bring the attention of the world on our problem. Bring the support of the world to bear on our side against Uncle Sam. Don't treat Uncle Sam like he's a friend. If he's a friend, we wouldn't be in this shape. If he was your friend, you wouldn't be a second-class citizen. If he was your friend, then a little black child wouldn't have been hung on a tree in Georgia the other day. If he was your friend, you wouldn't have a segregated school system in New York City. No, you have got no friends in Washington, D. C. You've only got friends when you get outside the confines of North America. You've got friends in Africa, friends in Asia, friends in Latin America.

So we have to take our problem to our friends, or put our problem at a level where our friends can help us or in a forum where our friends have some say-so. Since our friends abroad, our brothers, have no say-so in America's domestic affairs, we have to take our problem out of America's domestic jurisdiction and place it in a forum where our friends and our brothers have some say-so. In this we will be showing some intelligence because it will show that we are at least able to distinguish between friend and foe. Right now, we haven't always reflected this ability. We've gone to our enemy looking for friendship and we ran from our friends. They've put us on the racetrack.

We have to make the world see that the problem that we're confronted with is a problem for humanity. It's not a Negro problem; it's not an American problem. You and I have to make it a world problem, make the world aware that there'll be no peace on this earth as long as our human rights are being violated in America. Then the world will have to step in and try and see that our human rights are respected and recognized. We have to create a situation that will explode this world skyhigh unless we are heard from when we ask for some kind of recognition and respect as human beings. This is all we want—to be a human being. If we can't be recognized and respected as a human being, we have to create a situation where no human being will enjoy life, liberty, and the pursuit of happiness.

If you're not for that, you're not for freedom. It means you don't even want to be a human being. You don't want to pay the price that is necessary. And you shouldn't even be allowed around us other humans if you don't want to pay the price. You should be kept in the cotton patch where you're not a human being. You're an animal that belongs in the cotton patch like a horse and a cow, or a chicken or a possum, if you're not ready to pay the price that is necessary to be paid for recognition and respect as a human being.

Brothers, the price is death, really. The price to make others respect your human rights is death. You have to be ready to die or you have to be ready to take the lives of others. This is what old Patrick Henry meant when he said liberty or death. Life, liberty, the pursuit of happiness, or kill me. Treat me like a man, or kill me. This is what you have to say. Respect me, or put me to death. But when you start to put me to death, we're both going to die together. You have to say that.

This is not violence. This is intelligence. As soon as you start even thinking like that, they say you're advocating violence. No, you're advocating intelligence. Didn't you hear Lyndon B. Johnson last week when he said that they'll go to war in a minute to protect their life, liberty, and pursuit of happiness? Did they say LBJ was violent? No, they said he was a good president. Well, let's you and I be good presidents.

It's time for you and me now to let the world know how peaceful we are, how well-meaning we are, how law-abiding we wish to be. But at the same time we have to let the same world know we'll blow their world skyhigh if we're not respected and recognized and treated the same as other human beings are treated. If you won't tell them that, you need to just get off the planet. You shouldn't even be around in the company of people. No, in fact, you should be too ashamed to be seen out in public because you're not a man, you're less than a man, subhuman.

One of the first steps toward our being able to do this is to internationalize our problem. Let the world know that our problem is their problem, it's a problem for humanity. And the first form in which this can be done is the United Nations. One of the first acts of business of the Organization of Afro-American Unity is to organize the type of program that is necessary to take your and my case into the United Nations. Not only into the United Nations, but also we need to take it before every international body that sits on this earth. The Organization of African Unity, which consists of thirty-three independent African heads of state, will meet in Cairo on July 17. We should be there letting them know that we're catching hell in America.

If the Organization of African Unity is set up and composed of the independent heads of state from the African continent, and you and I are from Africa, have African blood in our veins, and we've heard them say that Africa is not free until all Africans are free — we're

Africans too, and we want them to be just as concerned
at the governmental level with our problem as they are
with the problems of our people in South Africa and
Angola. And we should let them know about it. . . .

Our problem should be placed before the Organization
of American States, the OAS. If they are going to listen
to the troubles that Cuba creates, if they are going to
take the trouble that Haiti presents to the Western Hemisphere before the OAS, if they take the Panamanian
situation before the OAS, or if they have trouble in Santo
Domingo and it goes before the OAS, you tell me by
what right the plight of 22 million of our people here
cannot be brought before the OAS. It should be brought
before the OAS. . . .

Very quickly, we'll leave the international situation
alone for a moment and come to the local situation. If
the Organization of Afro-American Unity feels that the
problem of black people in this country is worthy of
being brought before the world court in order to bring
about world opinion on our side, is that all we have
in mind? No. When you're in the ring fighting a man,
you've got to fight him with long jabs and short upper-
cuts. You've got to be slapping him while you're jooging,
and jooging while you're slapping him. You have to
have a long-range and a short-range goal. President
Nkrumah was most right when he said, "Seek ye first
the political kingdom, and all other things shall be added
unto it." This is good and true. Politics is power, the
science of how to govern.

The only real power that is respected in this society
is political power and economic power. Nothing else.
There's no such thing as a moral force that this government recognizes. Why, you're in a dream world. They
don't know what a moral force is. You read more about
moral corruption in Washington, D. C., than anything
else. Don't talk about what happened in Britain with
Christine Keeler. What's happening in Washington, D. C.?
Things that can't even be talked about. The only thing
in Britain is they bring it out in the open. The corrupters
in Washington are so powerful they can keep it from

coming out in the open because they've got something
on everybody. Everybody is in on it.

The only type of power that this government recognizes is political power and economic power. These are
the only two kinds. In the past, our leaders have shown
their lack of insight by not realizing that this segregated
school system was producing children with an inferior
education so that after they would graduate they still
weren't qualified to participate or compete. What have
we wasted our time doing? Protesting. To whom?
Donovan. Who else? Gross. Why? Because we didn't know
any better. Does Donovan hire himself? No. Does Gross
hire himself? No. Who hires both of them? The mayor.
We've been protesting against the puppet. Well, if you
want to protest you got to go against the puppeteer.
You have to strike at Wagner. How can you say Wagner is a good man and the two men he appointed are
bad men? Wagner isn't carrying out their program.
They're carrying out his program.

[*A passage is lost as tape is turned.*]

And the only way you can strike at him, you have to
have political power. How do we get political power?
We have to organize the people of Harlem in a door-
by-door campaign, I mean door by door, house by
house, people by people, person by person, and you
have to make them feel so ashamed that they're not
registered they won't even come out of the house. We
have to create an atmosphere in Harlem—and when
I say Harlem, the greater New York area—in which
every black man in the greater New York area will
feel like he's a traitor if he's not a registered voter.
His ballot will be like a bullet.

One or the other, we're at a time in history now where
we want freedom, and only two things bring you freedom—the ballot or the bullet. Only two things. Well,
if you and I don't use the ballot and get it, we're going
to be forced to used the bullet. And if you don't want
to use the ballot, I know you don't want to use the
bullet. So let us try the ballot. And if the ballot doesn't
work, we'll try something else. But let us try the ballot.

And the only way we can try the ballot is to organize
and put on a campaign that will create a new climate.

The Organization of Afro-American Unity is planning
a campaign that will enable us within a matter of weeks
to map out the city and touch every person in it who
looks like us. There's only one thing we want them to
do: register. That's all. We'll make it easy for them. Not
register as a Democrat or a Republican, but as an independent. Don't sell your soul. If you're registered as
a Democrat or a Republican, you've sold your soul.

An example. One of the worst things that anyone could
have done was done by a well-known Negro leader, so-
called — oh, I guess he's a Negro leader — when he condemned Goldwater. Tell you why. If he's already condemned Goldwater, what does Johnson have to do for
you now? Nothing. Don't let the man know what you're
against or who you're against. It's tactical suicide, tactical suicide, to let Lyndon B. Johnson know this far
in advance that you don't go for the man he's running
against. Why, he doesn't have to promise you anything.
He's already got you, dumb you, in his pocket. He
needs to offer nothing. Well, as long as you and I follow
that kind of birdbrain leadership, we never will have any
political haven. We'll have political hell. I'm not saying
that to criticize any personality, but it must be said. Before you and I commit ourselves in any kind of campaign, make sure that it's going to help the whole, or
don't say anything at all.

This doesn't mean that I'm for the man. But I never
let this man know that I'm against that man until I find
out what this man is putting down. Do you understand?
Don't let one think that he's got you in his pocket. Let
him know that he doesn't know which way you're going
until he produces something that is worthy of your support. Do you understand?

The no-knock law, the stop-and-frisk — we can go pick-
et the police station. What good will it do? The police
didn't pass the law. They're just out here. Who passed
the law? The legislators. How do you protest against
the legislators? With the ballot. So what the Negro lead-

er has had you and me doing is going in the wrong direction. Don't protest against the puppet. Go work on the puppeteer. Go get the director of the show and take him off the scene, and then you can change the cast or you can change the script.

The City Council right now is considering a law that's designed to make it illegal for you to walk with a rifle or have a rifle. Why just now? As long as it's been legal to own a rifle, why all of a sudden does the great white father want to pass a law making rifle-carrying illegal? Because of you; he's afraid of you getting rifles. Every law that they pass is aimed at you. Every legislator who walks inside the place where they make these laws, they think about you. They argue all night long on other laws. But when it comes to passing a law designed to keep you and me in the corral, they can pass it just like that.

So if you want to protest the no-knock law, you need the ballot. If you want to protest what the City Council is doing, you need the ballot. If you want to protest the segregated school system and change it, you need the ballot. Anything you can think of that you want to change right now, the only way you can change it is with a ballot or a bullet. And if you're not ready to get involved with either one of those, you are satisfied with the status quo. That means we'll have to change you.

There are 915,743 of our people in the state of Mississippi. That's almost a million. In 125 counties of Mississippi, they're in the majority. Ninety other counties, they constitute more than 40 percent of the population. Any time you have that number of black people who are of that numerical majority in that many counties, if they were given the vote, Eastland wouldn't be representing them. They'd be representing themselves. The state of Mississippi would be in the hands of the black man. And it must be in his hands—by the ballot or the bullet. It must be one or the other.

This is why the campaign that they have in Mississippi for voter registration is a good campaign. They're not trying to integrate, they're trying to get our people regis-

tered to vote, which is good, because it puts them in a
position to strike right at the base of all of their misery.
If our people down there are risking their lives so that
they can register and be in a position to vote or have
some say-so in their own destiny, what do you and I
look like in New York City, with the registration booth
only a few blocks away, and we haven't been in it?

And I say, brothers, you're talking to a man who's
guilty of all of this. I've never tried to take part in anything political. Couldn't see it. For one thing, I was in
a religious organization that was talking about something coming by-and-by. And any time you start thinking about something by-and-by, you can't take hold
of anything now-and-now or here-and-here. A lot of the
critics, civil rights persons, used to criticize us, especially me, for not being active in politics. They should be
glad, because so many of them were shamming and jiv-
ing — excuse the expression, but that's what they were
doing. When we get involved, we're involved for keeps.

We'll take a man and try and get all the people to
back him. But then if he sells us out, we'll put him in
the Hudson River. In the Hudson River, yes. We'll back
him, we'll support him, but he has to represent us, not
the man downtown. As soon as you back a man, you
put him in office, you put him in a position to get you
and me something, and then he starts dilly-dallying and
compromising and looking out for himself, why, the
very law of nature demands that that person be removed
by any means necessary.

Since our people are making such a sacrifice to become registered voters in Mississippi, it's a sin for you
and me not to be registered so we can vote in New
York City and in New York State, or throughout the
North. Here in this state they have forty-one congressmen. Nineteen of these forty-one congressmen from this
state are from New York City. New York City is so big
that almost half of all of the legislators that leave this
state and go to Washington, D. C., come from New York
City. They say that the size of New York City is around
8 million people. And they say there's about a million

and a half black people. When they say there's a million and a half, that means there's 3 million, because they never let you and me know how many there really are.

Out of the forty-one congressmen from this state, and the nineteen from New York City, only one is black. Think of it. Only one congressman, Adam Powell, out of all these black people, and you and I are saying hurray, hurray, hurray, we've got one. Why, brothers, we haven't got anything near what we're supposed to have. We become satisfied too quickly. We have to find out what enabled the people here in Manhattan to send a black man to Congress. Then let us see if the same situation exists in the Bronx and get a black man from the Bronx to go to Congress. And find out if the same situation that produced them exists in Brooklyn and get one from Brooklyn. Why, you're like a nut voting for someone to represent you in a legislative body who doesn't even look like you. Let us find out who is the congressman in every area where we live and then find out if he's serving us or if he's serving someone else. If he's serving us, let him stay there. And if he's not serving us, let us get rid of him.

Adam Powell is the only black politician in this country who is independent of the white political machine. This doesn't mean that he takes advantage of his position always for our good. And it doesn't mean by me saying this that I'm criticizing him. I'm not. I would never criticize him for the joy of white folks. They just go crazy when they hear you knock at Adam. If I thought he was wrong I wouldn't say so, I wouldn't give them that pleasure. In fact, I'd go for him as long as they don't go for him.

But the point that I'm trying to make is this, that he is independent of the political machine. Why? Because the people support him. Well, the people then should make him aware that *they* are aware that he wouldn't be there if it wasn't for them. And therefore the maximum mileage should be gotten from his position, maximum mileage. Because he's the only black politician in this country who's independent of the white political machine. And the only reason he's independent is because you support him. Most of these others — they have to rely on the machine in order to get in office. But once we find that we have a man that can buck the machine and still go to Washington, then we should let that man know that the only reason he's bucking it is because we're behind him. And if we're behind him, that means we're watching him and we want results.

There are two senators from this state. Neither one of them are black. Both of them pretend to be pro-black, but as politicians they don't dare to pretend to be anything else.

There are fifty-eight state senators. Out of those fifty-eight state senators, twenty-five come from New York City. And only two of them are black. Think of this. Twenty-five state senators from New York City and only two of them represent us.

There are 150 state assemblymen. Sixty-five of that 150 are from New York City. And out of that sixty-five, only four are black. Out of sixty-five, we have four. The state assembly is the one that passes the anti-Negro law, no-knock, stop-and-frisk. The state assembly, that's where it's passed. You don't protest at the police precinct. No, the law itself is opening the door for the cop to be a brute or to be a Gestapo-type policeman. But the man who makes this law is the one that goes up to Albany. You can keep him from going to Albany if you are a registered voter.

Once you get the ballot, you know what this means? You don't have to get out in the street any more and risk your health and your life and your limb demonstrating. All you have to do is organize that political power and direct it against anyone who's against you or direct it behind anyone who is for you. And in this way you and I will find that we're always taking constructive, positive action and getting some kind of result.

City councilmen, there are thirty-five city councilmen in New York City. Do you know out of thirty-five city councilmen, there's only one black one, and he's a coun-

cilman-at-large, J. Raymond Jones? And many of our
people don't even know who the black councilman is.
How would you expect to change our miserable situation when we have a council that the black man can't
even get into? He's not even represented there. We're not
represented in the city government in proportion to our
number. We're not represented in the state government
in proportion to our number. And we aren't represented
in the federal government in proportion to our number.

So, the only way we can get them to change their
laws is by becoming involved with the ballot. If the
ballot won't do it, there's no other alternative but the
bullet. I say there's no other alternative but the bullet.
As old Patrick Henry said — I always like to quote Pat
because when I was going to their school they taught
me to believe in it. They said he was a patriot. And
he's the only one I quote. I don't know what any of
the rest of them said. But I know what Pat said: Liberty or death. That means the ballot or the bullet. That's
what it means in Harlemese, in Harlem talk.

Again, some facts and figures on Harlem that will
only take a minute. The total black population based
on the 1960 census is 336,364 right here in Harlem.
In central Harlem between 110th Street and 155th Street,
there are supposedly 193,800 of our people. How do
they know? That's how many they counted. I've never
been counted. Most of you have never been counted.
How many of you have been at home when the man
came and said I'm a census taker? I want to see. Look
how many of you have your hand up. I know you
haven't been counted.

Well, how does the man know how many of us there
are? He doesn't know. He guesses, brothers. And he tells
you what he wants you to believe. Whenever you hear
this man tell you that there's 300,000, there's a million. He won't let you know how large you are or how
many of you there are. And I have never met anybody
yet that's been counted. Every once in a while, he runs
through the neighborhood and says yes, there's so many
and so many. He says that there are approximately

250,000 or more people eligible to register to vote. Approximately 125,000 are registered. Only 59,000 in the last congressional election. Less that 15,000 voted in the Democratic primary election. This shows you that most of our people don't involve themselves in politics at all. And if they did become involved and had a say-so in their destiny, everything would be a great deal different.

Another quick fact. It says that there are more than 10,000 people unemployed in central Harlem and there is not one employment office to accommodate them. Listen to this. The area of highest unemployment in the city is Harlem. There's not one employment office in Harlem. There are employment agencies. But there's a difference between an agency and an employment office. An agency sells you a job. If they get you a job, you've got to give them four months' pay. You work for them. That's slavery, brothers.

Why isn't there an employment office in Harlem if Harlem has the highest rate of unemployment? Can you see the conspiracy?

What the man does is, he sends you to the agency; you pay for your job, which means that if he gives you the job you've got to give him a cut for two months. As soon as your two months' work is up, the man fires you. This is a game, it's a conspiracy, between the employer and the employment agency. How many of you know that this is not true? This is true. They sell you a job. Then after they sell you a job, they fire you and sell that same job to somebody else. Why, brothers, it's time for you and me to go on the warpath behind what's coming down.

No, I say that this is bad. Women constitute 48 percent of the work force in Harlem, 48 percent of the work force. Women, your and my women. The man won't give us a job, he gives them a job washing his dishes and his little snotty-nosed blue-eyed babies. We go and take care of them.

Concerning the income in Harlem. The average family income in Harlem is only $3,723 per year. And it says here that a mayor's committee estimated that it takes

$6,000 per family to survive. Not to live in ease, to survive. Look, if the mayor sets up a committee and that committee does some research and comes up with the scientific finding that it takes $6,000 for the average family to survive, and then they say that you only average a little over $3,700, brothers, you're not surviving — you're in bad shape.

Approximately 15,000 in central Harlem receive some sort of public assistance. That means welfare.

There are 3,898 retail stores, all owned by whites, practically. They do an annual gross sale of $345,871,000 per year in this area. Meaning his businesses do this much gross sales in our neighborhood. Then he gives $10 back to the NAACP and $1 to CORE and tells you what a good man he is, he's your friend. Why, we need to wake up.

One hundred and sixty-eight liquor stores do an annual gross sale of $34,368,000. And this doesn't include bars and taverns. Did you hear what I said? The liquor store where you go and buy it by the bottle, not the nightclub or the bar or the tavern, but just the liquor store alone sells you $34,368,000 worth of whiskey a year. Why, you should be ashamed of your drunk self. Do you know that there are governments in Africa whose annual budget to run their entire country for the year isn't as much as you spend in central Harlem for whiskey? And you wonder why you're catching so much hell. Why, the money you spend for whiskey will run a government.

So we have to do something about this. And we intend to do it with the Organization of Afro-American Unity. And before we go a step farther — and we didn't intend to go this late tonight — we want to stop right now just before our question period and give Brother Benjamin here a chance to get on with our collection period. The reason we always have a collection period is that our public collection foots all of our expenses toward putting on these rallies . . . .

[*Collection is taken.*]

Question: (about John Brown)

Malcolm: Brother, yes, I understand what you're say-

ing, I think. There's an old African proverb which I find
most enlightening, which says that the enemy of my enemy is my friend. The enemy of my enemy is my friend.
As long as there's a lion coming after me, if I'm throwing stones at it and you're throwing chickens at it and
someone else is throwing something else at it, as long
as everybody else throws something at it, as far as I'm
concerned they're all right with me, at least at this time.
And if things change, then things will change. If the situation changes, everything changes. But as long as
they're throwing something at the lion, we say good.

This doesn't mean that you always trust your allies.
But as long as they want to ally themselves against the
same one that you're fighting against, watch them and
let them go ahead and fight against it. Yes, sir?

Question: Are there any fallout shelters in Harlem?

Malcolm: Brother, if anything ever happens where
you need a fallout shelter, a fallout shelter won't do you
any good. When things get that bad, a fallout shelter
won't do you any good. When things get that bad, forget it. And they are heading in that direction. Yes, sir?

Question: Brother teacher, must we utilize John Brown
as a friend of the black man?

Malcolm: No, I don't say he was a friend of the black
man. I use it to give you an example of how to test the
white man who says he's your friend. Let him go down
with some action similar to John Brown's. If he's willing
to die for you and all of that, then let him go ahead
and do it.

Same questioner: (about other whites who had been
friendly to the Negro)

Malcolm: You said they were friendly, but you didn't
say they were friends. There's a difference.

Same questioner: Well, they didn't give their life but
they did great things to help.

Malcolm: Whatever good they did, good. But we don't
have to blow the bugle for any of them. We don't have
to blow the bugle. Look, I've got an example. Some
of them have died right now in Mississippi to try and
change the situation. We still don't need to blow the

bugle because the situation is there still. We don't blow any bugles until the war's over. All the dying that they do is for naught if the situation remains the same. Some of us get too happy at an opportunity to find good white folks. Whatever good they do, good. If you want to use it as an example, good. But don't blow the bugle over it. And any time you find white people who help you just so you can say you're a good white man, no. Yes, ma'am?

Question: Where can you join the bullet campaign?

Malcolm: Just join the Organization of Afro-American Unity. If you're interested in action, the Organization of Afro-American Unity has departments for any kind of action you want. If you want ballot action, we have that political department. If you want business action, we have a department that you can get involved in that will enable you to show us how to develop businesses and solve some of our economic problems. If you're interested in the cultural department, we have that. If you're interested in other departments, we also have them. Some of them we don't list publicly.

But I might point out you would be very surprised and encouraged to know how many of our people there are who are ready and willing to become involved actively in any kind of physical campaign designed to bring about an end to the Klan and these other racists who have been brutalizing our people. You have black people, we've had over 400 of them who have telephoned just within the past week to find out when you're going, [saying] count me in. Yes, sir?

Question: (says there is also a Negro city councilman from Brooklyn)

Malcolm: Very good, brother. I'm sorry they didn't give me that information. So that means there are two out of twenty-five. And they're so quiet we never even heard their names.

Why, don't you know when a black man goes downtown and represents us, he's supposed to be like Powell? Powell's the loudest thing in this country. That's why they don't like him. They don't dislike him because he goes to Europe, because *they* go to Europe. All that other stuff that they say about him, they're not against him because of that. They're against him because he's loud.

And in the history of this country polite black people have never been successful in bringing about any kind of advantages for black people. You have to walk in with a hand grenade and tell the man, listen, you give us what we've got coming or nobody is going to get anything. Then he might listen to you. But if you go in there polite and acting responsible and sane, why, you're wasting your time, you have to be insane. Yes, brother?

Question: Brother Malcolm, do you think it's wise that we should make it publicly known that possibly guerrillas are going to Mississippi or other places so the white man can be prepared—

Malcolm: He's already prepared, brother. He's already prepared. Sometimes it is good. If the United States government doesn't want you and me going into Mississippi organizing our people into the type of units that will enable them to retaliate against the Ku Klux Klan and create a very nasty situation in this country for the whole world to see, then the government should occupy the state of Mississippi.

Same questioner: Well, don't you think the element of surprise would be better able to get the same thing done?

Malcolm: Before the Chinese came across the Yalu during the Korean war, they told Uncle Sam, don't come another step, or else we're going to do such and such a thing. They were so confident in their ability to take on anything Sam had, they said don't come another step or we're going to do thus and so.

Brother, let me tell you about a Klansman. He's a coward. He can be thoroughly organized and if you go like that [*stamps his foot*], he'll cut out. That's why they're hiding beneath those sheets. You never read where *a* Klansman does anything, you read where the mob does so and so. Because they're cowards. Any time

you get black people to take a stand against those sheet-
ed so-called knights, you'll get rid of them overnight.
And I for one would announce yes, we are doing it,
and get some black people and go on down there. And
I don't think we'd be the loser, no.

In fact, I know we wouldn't. We've got black people
in Mississippi right now who are already ready. They
are already ready, they are sitting there waiting. The
white man is finding out they've authorized it a long
time ago. They're waiting for someone to let them know
that it's all right. See, the preacher has been telling them
that it's not all right. And once you make it known that
it's all right to fight to defend yourself, that it's your
right, that you are justified in returning bullet for bullet
with a racist organization like the Klan—let them know
it, and you won't even have to go down there. There's
enough of them there to do it themselves. But you want
to be in on the action. I'm telling you, Harlem is full
of our people who want to go down there. Some of them
come from down there. Yes, sir?

Question: Brother Malcolm, I was reading the *Amsterdam News* on the way to this meeting. And they have
an article in there that says Malcolm X offers his assistance to CORE and these other supposedly nonviolent
organizations. In this article they said that they were
considering your offer but they hadn't made any comment about it yet. I'd like for you to read the article.

Malcolm: We don't have time to read the whole article. We're glad you gave the *Amsterdam News* a plug.
And tell them that you gave them a plug so they'll mention in their next week's edition that we're going to have
a rally next Sunday.

We sent a telegram to the Student Nonviolent Committee in Mississippi, telling them that if the federal government won't protect the lives and the property of our
people that we would send some brothers down there
who knew how to organize our people into self-defense
units that would show our people how to speak the
only language that the Klan understands. And the only
language they understand is the language of force. I'm

telling you: Anytime you lay a few Klansmen out, dead, the government will step in.

Now, am I supposed to be charged with advocating violence? Let me show you what a rotten system this is. They'll walk out of here and say I'm advocating violence. They won't say that the Klan is practicing violence, they won't say that the White Citizens Council is practicing violence, they won't say that the United States government is condoning violence. All they'll do is walk out and say we are advocating violence. You're living in a rotten system. No, we should declare open season on Klansmen, open season. Let it be known. Yes, ma'am . . .

Question: How can you register as an independent when there's no independent party?

Malcolm: A person can register as an independent voter and then vote any way they want. No, I'm not speaking of an independent party. I'm speaking of a person registering as an independent voter, meaning that you're not committed to any party. . . .

Question: What can the people who are already registered Democrat or Republican do? You talk about those who should register. But what about those who are registered as Democrats or Republicans?

Malcolm: You have no problem. You can easily become an independent registered voter. If you were a Democrat, you could become a Republican, couldn't you? If you were a Republican, you could change your party affiliation to Democrat.

Question: But if I am registered as a Democrat, what should I do?

Malcolm: Get with the rest of the independent voters. All I'm trying to show you is that we need a collective body of registered voters who are not committed to any party and not committed to any man until we find out what we're going to receive from that commitment, some positive results from that commitment.

Question: But how can you uncommit yourself?

Malcolm: If you're already committed? We'll look into it and let you know next week. And that's one of the reasons why we have a political committee, which we feel will have the type of political know-how to steer us around any problem that we're confronted by. It's best to be uncommitted. A black man that's committed is out of his mind. Be uncommitted. Because you haven't thrown a punch doesn't mean you can't throw it. And as long as you haven't thrown it, you've always got one to throw. Yes, ma'am?

Question: Brother Malcolm, just a comment: all we have to know is what Adam Powell has been doing the past few years.

Malcolm: He jumped from party to party, didn't he? But we want to give an explanation so that it will be clarified. We can best give you one by having our committee that has that responsibility get that information. And at our meeting next Sunday night we'll have that. Yes, ma'am?

Question: (about getting an appointment to discuss a problem)

Malcolm: You can get it right at the [Hotel] Theresa office. Make it through the secretary there. I don't run from people. But the reason that I never make far-in-advance appointments is because I don't want a situation to ever come up where I have to stand somebody up. Right now, things are pretty hot for me, you know. Oh, yes.

I'm trying to stay alive, you understand. I may sound like I'm cracking, but I'm facting. I've been hinting for two months what it was all about and some people thought I was crazy. But some of it's beginning to come out now. And the white press didn't bring it out. They sat on it because they didn't want that thing to crumble. Any time they find that something is putting black people in a vise, they want that thing to exist. If you notice, anything as a rule that is written up — again, like the *Journal American* did last Sunday; they said that we had 600 people out here. See, they're chronic liars. And they said what an overwhelming victory was scored by Elijah Muhammad.

Well, you know, I hate to get on this subject. You all

will forgive me if I do. But they said that they expected
500,000 at the Armory. And if they had 10,000, why,
good night, they're still 490,000 short, unless their public relations man made a typographical error when he
was putting out the press release. So I don't call that
any kind of victory. But they like to use us one against
the other. That's really what they're trying to do. And
sometimes you find us, we're dumb enough to let ourselves be used one against the other. So, the secretary
there at the office in the Theresa will set that up. There,
'way in the back —

Question: You once stated that the only solution for
the so-called Negro was ultimately to return to Africa.
Then at the last meeting, you said we should turn to
Africa culturally and spiritually, but politically should
stay in this country.

Malcolm: Hold it right there. The first statement that
I made, I made before going to Africa myself. I spent
about five weeks over there speaking to every kind of
African leader that I could gain access to. And the net
result of that trip was that if our people go, they're welcome. But those who are politically mature over there
say that we would be wiser to play a role at this time
right here. If we want to go back, we're welcome, but
what we do should be for the good of the whole, not
for the few. Any time you restore cultural or spiritual
bonds between our people here and our people there,
then we begin to work together. Right now, someone is
needed right here to do some work for the whole. And
you and I are in the best position to do it.

Same questioner: (remarks not audible)

Malcolm: Brother, if all of us wanted to go back to
Africa — you wouldn't be satisfied to go back all by
yourself, I know that. Your desire would be to see all
of us go back if I am judging you correctly. Then how
would you create a situation, number one, that would
make all of us black-minded enough to want to go
back, or make all of us have a thorough enough knowledge of what it is like over there to want to go back,
or make this man so fed up with us he'd want to send
us there? How would you go about doing it? How would

you go about getting 22 million people to go to a place that they think is a rotten, insect-infested jungle? How would you go about getting them to go back when they cringe when you use the word African or Africa? What strategy would you use? Or else you'd end up going back by yourself.

Don't you know you've got some nationalists right here that aren't ready to go back? They'll talk that talk, I mean talk that talk, but when it comes to taking some concrete action, that's just talk. Well, let's face reality. Our people have to be brought up to the point where we have sufficient understanding of the assets that are due us if we do go back. And as long as you can't get 22 million people to that level or to that point, then while you are trying to point them in that direction, you have to at the same time have some kind of program which will enable them to take the maximum advantage of every opportunity that exists here.

I want to go back to Africa. But what can I do while I'm waiting to go? Go hungry? Live in a rat-infested slum? Send my children to a school where their brains are being crippled? No, if we are going to go but time is going to pass between now and our going, then we have to have a long-range program and a short-range program, one that is designed to turn us in that direction, but at the same time one that is designed to enable us to take maximum advantage of every opportunity under this roof where we are right now. One more question — yes, sir?

Question: What will be the attitude of this organization toward American intervention in Africa?

Malcolm: The brother wants to know what will be the attitude of this organization in regards to American intervention in Africa. By that you're probably referring to recently, when they bombed our Congolese brothers, when American pilots bombed our brothers in the Congo. Why, that was worse than what the Italians did to our brothers in Ethiopia.

Any time these kinds of things take place, you and I should be organized in such a way that the American government will think a long time before it takes any steps towards dropping bombs on Africans who are our brothers and sisters. This is why we must organize. But this handful of people here means nothing. We have to organize ourselves and then organize the city and then organize the state and then organize the country. Once you do this, the government is not going to intervene in Africa.

Walking downtown with a sign saying we protest what you did in the Congo means nothing if you're not organized. We have to organize house by house, street by street, city by city, state by state, every black man of African descent in the Western Hemisphere. And then you and I can stop the acts of atrocity not only in Mississippi, but also in the Congo. But first you have to organize. Coming to these meetings is not organization. After coming, go back and take out a membership so that we can get organized, and so at these membership meetings we can then tell you how you can help us organize others. And then if those organize others and those organize others, the first thing you know we'll have this city organized. *Then* you can act.

Other than that, everything is premature, it is actually premature. You protest, you feel good, your chest is out. But what do you get? Nothing. Because, brothers, the man studies all these actions before he makes his move. When you see them intervening in the Congo and then have nerve enough to tell the press, so that they'll tell the American public — proof of which, name me a Negro paper that protested. Name a Negro — I use the word Negro now on purpose — name a Negro organization that protested. Name a Negro leader that protested. The State Department knew in advance what it was doing. They're not worried about those organizations, or those leaders. But this handful of people [here] means nothing. What you and I have to do is organize, organize every black face you can find. And I'll guarantee you that they'll know in advance if we're organized, before they make any move in the Congo or anywhere else.

But one of the worst slaps in the face that the black man in this country has received was when the State

Department had the audacity last week to admit that American pilots were bombing defenseless Africans in the Congo. And not one outcry was made among our people. The Negro leaders are too busy talking about rowdyism on the subways. Pick up on that. Rowdyism among Negroes on the subway, and black people are being torn from limb to limb by American bombs dropped by American pilots from American planes. Last question.

[*Tape ends as questioner starts to tell about personal harassment by the police in the Bronx.*]

6 A LETTER FROM CAIRO

At the OAAU's July 5 rally, Malcolm X urged the audience to attend the next rally on July 12, but he himself was not present. On July 5 he also noted that the Organization of African Unity was to meet in Cairo on July 17 and said, "We should be there letting them know that we're catching hell in America." Malcolm was there—recognized as an observer at the OAU conference—and he submitted a memorandum circulated to the participants, letting them know that the recently enacted civil rights law had not seriously changed conditions for Afro-Americans, and appealing for their support in his moves to indict the United States government before the United Nations. (See Malcolm X Speaks for the text of the memorandum, which is often erroneously referred to as a speech.)

Malcolm left New York on July 9 and did not return until November 24. He spent most of the first half of this time in Cairo, and most of the second half visiting other countries in Africa. He kept notes about his travels and discussions, hoping to be able to write a *book about them, but little has been written about this period (and some of the little written is more fiction than fact).*

The following letter is the only item in this book from Malcolm's second African trip in 1964. Despite its brevity, it is highly revealing — not about the African experience, but about Malcolm, his character, his developing views, and his relations with his movement.

The letter reflects his intense concern with internationalizing the struggle, and his awareness of the personal dangers this meant for him. It also testifies to his modesty, his objectivity and his unceasing desire to learn and grow ("the problem . . . is bigger and more complicated than many of us realize").

In addition, it offers evidence about the kind of movement he was trying to build in his last year. He wanted a movement that would not merely be different from the Nation of Islam (and from other organizations created after his death ostensibly in his name and tradition). What he sought was a movement that would be free of leadership cultism, where the members would be able to express differences and grievances, and where the leaders would be responsible to the members. That is, a democratic as well as a revolutionary movement.

In this chapter, the use of three periods (. . .) is Malcolm's, and does not represent omissions.

The letter was originally printed in a mimeographed Harlem publication, Black Force, *undated but issued around early 1967.*

Cairo, Egypt
August 29, 1964

As-Salaam Alaikum.
In the name of *Allah*, the Beneficent, the Merciful . . .
My Dear Brothers and Sisters:
My stay here in Egypt is just about drawing to a close; my mission here in your behalf is just about complete in this part of Africa. For the next few weeks, unless something drastic happens to force me to change

my plans, I will be traveling through several other African countries visiting and speaking in person to various
African leaders at all levels of government and society,
giving them a firsthand knowledge and understanding
of our problems, so that all of them will see, without
reservation, the necessity of bringing our problem before the United Nations this year, and why we must
have their support.

I'm not at all doubtful of support, but I've learned
that one cannot take things for granted and then cry
when nothing materializes. We must learn that we are
masters of our own destiny, but only when we exercise
the maximum efforts to get things done. Take nothing
for granted in this world and we will then be assured
of success.

You must realize that what I am trying to do is very
dangerous, because it is a direct threat to the entire
international system of racist exploitation. It is a threat
to discrimination in all its international forms. Therefore, if I die or am killed before making it back to the
States, you can rest assured that what I've already set
in motion will never be stopped. The foundation has
been laid and no one can hardly undo it. Our problem has been *internationalized*. The results of what I
am doing will materialize in the future and then all of
you will be able to see why it is necessary for me to
be here this long and what I was laying the foundation for while here.

I have been pleased to receive letters from many of
you lately, especially to know that you would take time
from your many other duties and obligations to write
to me. From the sound of some of the letters there seems
to be much dissatisfaction and disunity creeping in among
you, and some seem dissatisfied even with me. This
sounds like history repeating itself. I want you to know
that this is normal, and therefore it doesn't excite or
worry me. I'm not particularly surprised at the ones
around whom so much of the controversy and dissatisfaction seems to be raging, because experience has taught
me never to take anyone or anything for granted.

Being away from America is a blessing in more ways than one; it has enabled me to become untangled from the strong emotional issues and step back and view the whole picture with more objectivity than I could if I were right there. I can even see the problems better that have risen within our own OAAU and the Muslim Mosque.

Let me restate my own position: I believe in human rights for everyone, and that none of us is qualified to judge each other, and that none of us should therefore have that authority. We don't have the right to force anyone to walk with us, nor do we have the right to condemn those who want to leave, those who become impatient when they don't see us getting results and therefore want to try another way. We can't blame them, and we have no right to be angry with them. If we ourselves produce results, people will stay and they will all support a good program that is getting good results.

If brothers want to establish another organization, even that is their right. We must learn to wish them well, and mean it. Our fight must never be against each other. No matter how much we differ over minor things, our fight must always be directed against the *common enemy*.

If any Muslims are dissatisfied they cannot be compelled to stay among us, and cannot be condemned for leaving us. This is the point I'm trying to get across to you. I only say that those of you who do go, try to keep good thoughts in your heart about us, for we shall be trying to think good things about you.

If any of you want to leave the OAAU and form something else, I say the same to you that I say to the Muslims. But wherever you go and whatever you do, remember that we are all still brothers and sisters and we still have the same problem. Let us not waste time condemning and fighting each other. We have already wasted too much time and energy doing this in the past.

I know your grievances, much of which is just, but much of which is also based upon inability to look at the problem as a *whole*. It is bigger and more complicated than many of us realize. I've never sought to be anyone's leader. There are some of you there who want leadership. I've stayed away this summer and given all those who want to show what they can do the opportunity to do so. When I return I will work with anyone who thinks he can lead . . . and I only pray to *Allah* that you will work with me likewise.

I hope my position is clear: I'm not interested in fighting Elijah Muhammad or any other Afro-American. I don't even want any arguments with them. If our own program produces results then our work will speak for itself. If we don't produce results then we have no argument anyway. Brother Benjamin is the best teacher I left behind: he has many faults and many weaknesses, but then so have I and so have many of the rest of you.

I'm going to be away for at least another month. During that time you can overlook the small differences that you have and make progress by working with each other, or you can be at odds and make no progress. You can make the Muslim Mosque and OAAU a success, or you can destroy both organizations. It's up to you. You have one more month. I have so much faith in *Allah*, and in *right*, and in my people, that I believe I can come back and start from scratch if it is necessary and as long as I mean right *Allah* will bless me with success and our people will help me in this fight. I love all of you, and pray *Allah* will bless all of you.

Salaam Alaikum,
Your brother and servant

7 AT A MEETING IN PARIS

On his way home from Africa, Malcolm X stopped off in Paris, where he spoke at the Salle de la Mutualité on November 23, 1964, at a meeting sponsored by "Présence Africaine," the African cultural organization. The only report of the meeting in the American press, by Ruth Porter, began as follows:

"There wasn't a square inch of unoccupied space in the meeting room. The seats were filled an hour before the lecture was scheduled to begin. The 'late' arrivals stood or sat on the floor. When not another human being could be jammed into the hall, the crowd spilled into the corridors, hoping to stand within earshot. Those who arrived on time could not find standing room in the corridors and had to leave. The speaker himself could barely push into the room over the assorted legs of those on the floor. Africans, Americans black and white, European leftists of all persuasions, representatives of the press, all were intensely interested in what Malcolm X would say." (The Militant, December 7, 1964)

Malcolm's opening remarks, printed under the title of

113

"The Black Struggle in the United States" in the English-language edition of Présence Africaine, *No. 2, 1965, are omitted here because they repeat material found elsewhere in this book, but the full text of his answers to twenty-four questions follows. In this chapter, three periods (. . .) represent gaps in the tape recording as transcribed by* Présence Africaine.

Question 1: How is it possible that some people are still preaching nonviolence?

Malcolm X: That's easy to understand—shows you the power of dollarism. The dollar makes anything possible. In nineteen-sixt— (I forget what year it was when the Sharpeville massacre took place in South Africa) if you read the testimony of Mandela in court, he brought out the fact that at that point the brothers in South Africa had begun to realize that they had to go into action, that nonviolence had become outdated: it only helped the enemy. But at the same time the enemy knows that once eleven million people stop being confined to a nonviolent approach against three million, you're going to have a different situation. They had to use their new modern tricks, so they ran down and got one of the Africans and gave him a glorious peace prize for being nonviolent, and it lent strength to the nonviolent image, to try and keep them a little nonviolent a little while longer. And it's the same way in the States. The black man in the States has begun to see that nonviolence is a trick that is put upon him to keep him from even being able to defend himself.

And so there's an increasing number of black people in America who are absolutely ready and willing to do whatever is necessary to see that their lives and their own property are protected by them.

So you have again your imperialists, and whatever else you call them, come along and give out another peace prize to again try and strengthen the image of nonviolence. This is their way of doing things, but everybody doesn't always accept those peace prizes.

Question 2: I should like to ask Mr. Malcolm X two questions. The first, what is his opinion of the Jewish problem and the solidarity of Jews and Negroes against racism? The second, if he knows the names of Lincoln, Wilberforce, Garrison, John Brown and others, and what is his opinion of these gentlemen?

Malcolm: Most white people who profess to be for the Negro struggle are usually with it as long as they are nonviolent. And they're the ones who encourage them to be nonviolent, to love their enemies, and turn the other cheek. But those who are genuinely for the freedom of the black man — as far as we're concerned, they're all right. Now in regards to what is my opinion of the Jews. I don't think that a man can be intelligent when he's in the frying pan and he becomes wrapped up or involved in trying to solve someone else's problems or cry for someone else. The American Negroes especially have been maneuvered into doing more crying for the Jews than they cry for themselves.

In America the Jews used to be segregated. They never were "Freedom Riders." They didn't use this tactic to solve their problem — begging in, walking in, wading in. Whenever they were barred from a neighborhood they pooled their economic power and purchased that neighborhood. If they were barred from hotels, they bought the hotel. But when they join us, they don't show us how to solve our problem that way. They show us how to wade in and crawl in and beg in. So I'm for the Jew when he shows me how to solve my problem like he has solved his problem.

Question 3: May I ask you if you were a Muslim before joining the "Black Muslims" or if you chose that religion after, and, if so — why?

Malcolm: A man's choice of religion is his personal business, but I might add to your question. Christianity was used in America on us, on our people, not to take us to Heaven but to make us good slaves, primarily — by robbing us of our right to defend ourselves in the name of Jesus.

Question 4: Many black Americans are hoping you

will be their leader. Do you have a determined political
program and I would like to know, if you do have a
political program which has already been set up, would
you join this with a new organization which is called
" Freedom Now"?

Malcolm: First, I don't profess to be anybody's leader.
I'm one of 22 million Afro-Americans, all of whom
have suffered the same things. And I probably cry out
a little louder against the suffering than most others and
therefore, perhaps, I'm better known.

I don't profess to have a political, economic, or social
solution to a problem as complicated as the one which
our people face in the States, but I am one of those
who is willing to try *any means necessary* to bring an
end to the injustices our people suffer.

One of the reasons why I say it's difficult to come
up and say "this is the solution" or "that is the solution"
is that a chicken cannot produce a duck egg, and it
can't produce a duck egg because the system itself was
produced by a chicken egg and can only reproduce
what produced it.

The American system was produced from the enslave-
ment of the black man. This political, economic, and
social system of America was produced from the en-
slavement of the black man and that particular system
is capable only of reproducing that out of which itself
was produced. The only way a chicken can produce
a duck egg [is] you have to revolutionize the system.

Question 5: The history of the United States has clearly
proved that none of the previous presidents has been
able to solve integration. Now I'd like to know, Mr.
Malcolm, your position in so far as the last election is
concerned and what do you think in particular of devel-
opments in the future under President Johnson?

Malcolm: It's the same system. It's not the President
who can help or hurt. And this system is not only ruling
us in America — it's ruling the world.

Nowadays when a man is running for president of
the United States he's not running for the president of
the United States alone, but he has to be acceptable to

every area of the world where the influence of the United States reaches. If Johnson had been running all by himself he wouldn't have been acceptable by himself. The only thing that made him acceptable to the world was the shrewd capitalists. The shrewd imperialists knew that the only way that you will voluntarily run to the fox is to show you a wolf. So they created a ghastly alternative and had the whole world, even the so-called intellectuals who call themselves Marxists and other things, hoping that Johnson would beat Goldwater.

I have to say this. Those who claim to be enemies of the system were on their hands and knees waiting for Johnson to get elected because he's supposed to be a man of peace; and he has troops invading the Congo right now and invading Saigon and places where other countries have pulled their troops out. Johnson is sending his troops in. I'm just telling you what I think of him. He sends Peace Corps to Nigeria and mercenaries to the Congo.

Question 6: As a solution to this problem can one envisage the creation of an independent black state in the United States?

Malcolm: No! I wouldn't say "No, No." I wouldn't close the door to any solution. Our problem in the States is so deplorable we are justified to try anything — *anything*. Other independent states have been set up. They set up Israel and they weren't called separationists. But when we start talking about setting up something wherein we can rule ourselves, we're labeled separationists. But we are not separationists, nor are we integrationists. We're human beings.

Question 7: Brother Malcolm, can you foresee the day when the Negro race and culture will be respected in the world and even be predominant?

Malcolm: If I understand your question, brother, I have to say "Yes." I see the time when the black culture will be the dominant culture and when the black man will be the dominant man. And nobody should be against the black man being the dominant man. He's been dominated. I don't think that if we allow ourselves to be

dominated it's wrong to pass the ball around once in
a while. We've served everyone else, probably more so
than anyone else has. We've permitted our continent to
be raped and ravaged. We've permitted over 100 million
human souls to be uprooted from the mother continent
and shipped abroad, many of whom lost their lives
at the bottom of the sea or were eaten by sharks. We've
contributed to the economy of every country on the face
of this earth with our slave labor. So if there's any
kind of justice, if there's any kind of judgment, if there's
any kind of God—then if he's coming to execute judgment or give some kind of justice—we have some bills
that we haven't collected yet.

Question 8: Are you against the love between a black
person and a white person?

Malcolm: How can anyone be against love? Whoever
a person wants to love that's their business—that's like
their religion.

Question 9 (same questioner): But you say "hate the
tree."

Malcolm: I haven't said anything about "hate the tree."
I said you can't help hating the roots and you hate the
roots—not hating the tree—and I said it in reference
to the way that they have taught us to hate our roots,
which means the African continent. Only many Negroes
don't know their roots—they think when you talk about
roots you're talking about Europe.

Question 10 (same questioner): Most Negroes in America are "sooners."

Malcolm: Mixed?

Questioner: Just as soon be one thing as another.

Malcolm: That's all through indoctrination, brainwash-
ing and training, but you'll find the Afro-American is
getting away from that now. There was a time—I'll
comment on that—when you would find the American
Negroes who'd be so proud of their white blood—and
not only American Negroes, but all over. But this was
only because Europe was in a position of power and it
served as a status symbol. But, if you notice, Europe
is losing its power. When Europe lost its grip in Asia

and Africa it upset the economy of these European countries, so that today they face a crisis — not only an economic crisis — they face a political crisis, a social crisis, a moral crisis, and even a military crisis. And so it's not a status symbol any more to be running around bragging about your Scotch blood or your German blood or this other kind of blood. Now the pendulum is changing in the other direction. You've got Europeans talking about that other kind of blood.

Question 11: Do you foresee a total assimilation with equal rights of the Afro-American into the white community of the United States in many, many years to come?

Malcolm: No! Nobody! Who's going to wait many years? I'm glad you asked the question like that because, you see, the oppressed never uses the same yardstick as the oppressor.

And this is what the oppressor doesn't realize. In his position of power he takes things for granted and he takes it for granted that everybody uses his yardstick. Well, today for a long time, we, the oppressed people, not only in America but in Africa, Asia and elsewhere, had to use someone else's yardstick. When they said "fast," what was "fast" to them was "fast" to us, but nowadays the yardstick has changed. We got our own yardstick. And when you say a long time this assimilation, or a long time this solution, the thing you don't realize is that other generations used a different yardstick. They had patience and you could tell them a long time and they would sit around a long time, but the young ones that's coming up now are asking "Why should he wait? Why should he have to wait for what other people have when they're born? Why should he have to go to a Supreme Court or to a Congress, or to a Senate, or to some kind of legislative body to be told he's a man when other people don't have to go through that process to be told that they're a man?" So you have a new generation coming up . . . necessary to let the world know right now that they're going to be men or there just won't be a human being anywhere else.

Question 12: Is there a Negro movement in the United States that wishes to form a Negro state with the Africans?

Malcolm: Yes, they are important. There are an increasing number of Afro-Americans who want to migrate back to Africa. Now if it were to take place tomorrow you would probably have a limited number. So, in my opinion, if you wanted to solve the problem you would have to make the problem more digestible to a greater number of Afro-Americans. The idea is good but those who propagated the idea in the past put it to the public in the wrong way and because of this didn't get the desired result. The one who made the greatest impact was the honorable Marcus Garvey. And the United States government . . . put him in prison and charged him with fraud.

A spiritual "Back-to-Africa." If our people would try to migrate back to Africa culturally, first try to migrate back culturally and philosophically and psychologically, they would stay where they are physically but this psychological, cultural, philosophical migration would give us bonds with our mother continent that would strengthen our position in the country where we are right now, and then we'd be in a position to influence that government's policies and keep them from supporting men like Tshombe.

Question 13: Brother Malcolm, don't you think there is a danger in the United States that the Negroes will become diluted in the white majority?

Malcolm: Yes, brother, it does represent that danger but you can't ever have integration. They will never have integration in that country. Right now, if a Negro moves into a neighborhood, the white liberals are the first ones to move out. They can't integrate the schools in New York City. The United Nations diplomats are complaining that they're getting a beating for no other reason than their skin is dark — in New York City, not Mississippi. Integration would destroy our people, but we'll never have it in that country.

Question 14: Why doesn't Mr. Malcolm X utilize his influence to prevent black athletes from taking part in the Olympic games?

Malcolm: They're athletes. If they didn't participate you wouldn't even see America in the Olympics. Anything that they've let us do, we do it better than they.

Question 15: Does he believe truly in the birth of the black man, such as he described it in his autobiography?

Malcolm: No, I didn't describe it. It was wrongly worded by the writer. If you read it closely, you will find that this was a story being told to me and it wasn't about the birth of the black man, it was the birth of the white man.

You can't find the beginning of the black man. Anywhere you go you find the black man, but you do find the time when the whites seemed to be making their appearance on the scene. When you go back into your ancient history usually you deal with dark-skinned peoples. Most of your archaeologists, delving in the remains of ancient civilizations, spend most of their time in Africa and Asia, seldom in Europe. This doesn't take away from the European, but most of the ancient civilizations that were highly developed were in Asia and Africa. So there's more evidence to support the ancient past of the people in Africa and Asia; but when you go back into the European area you usually end up in caves.

Question 16: Mr. Malcolm X, can you tell us at this very moment how you plan to present the problem of the Afro-American to international juridical bodies and the United Nations?

Malcolm: I would not say how we plan. I would not say publicly how I plan to do anything. The only thing that's necessary to get is the assistance of any independent African nation or Asian nation or European nation that's a member of the United Nations.

Now it would be a sin (or, as in Harlem we say, "a drag") if, with all of the independent African nations, 22 million Afro-Americans would have difficulty getting their problems into the United Nations. It would put someone on the spot. I have seen the statesmen in the UN debating the South African question, crying at the top of their voices over the inhuman treatment, and come back to their hotel room and turn on the TV

and look at the news and see Negroes, right there where
the UN is, being bitten by dogs and having their skulls
crushed by police clubs and the clothing ripped from
their bodies by water hoses, and walk back in the UN
the next day and say nothing about it. You can't tell
me anything about South Africa, Mozambique, Angola,
or anywhere and make me believe you're sincere as
long as you keep quiet about what the United States
is doing to us in that country.

Question 17: Mr. Malcolm, you want to form a movement which is extremist, and you have said that there
must be a movement of Afro-Americans towards Africa — a philosophical, psychological and cultural return — but that the struggle must take place in the United
States. Consequently, in the event where the Afro-Americans' demands are not satisfied, what means do they
think of using to make an eventual return to Africa?

Malcolm: What country are you from?

Answer: Senegal.

A Voice: That is not the opinion of all Senegalese.

Malcolm: Number one, if we are extremists we're not
ashamed of it. In fact, the conditions that our people
suffer are extreme and an extreme illness cannot be
cured with a moderate medicine. We're not against physical migration of our people back to Africa. Those who
want to go back and have something to contribute to
the development of Africa, we are for them, because we
feel a strong Africa makes us strong also.

To the same degree Africa is independent and respected we are independent and respected, but to the degree
we are disrespected the Africans are also disrespected.
Our origin is the same and our destiny is the same,
whether we like it or not.

Those of us in the West were sold. We didn't sell ourselves. This is the point we want our brothers, when
they're judging us, always to keep in their minds. We
didn't go to America voluntarily. We were sold there,
and some of those who sold us were our friends, and
some of those who sold us were our relatives. In the
Bible and in the Koran there is a story about a man

named Joseph who was sold into slavery by his brothers, but he forgave his brothers who sold him into slavery because he was in a position to forgive them.

Question 18: Malcolm, in the same way you said that there were certain Negroes who had helped and assisted in the sale of their own brothers . . .

Malcolm: I didn't say that like that. Before you get into that I want to remind you of something. Joseph forgave his brothers. Nothing in there where they forgave Pharaoh who purchased him — enslaved him. The country that bought him and enslaved him was destroyed.

Question 19 (same questioner): If it was our white ancestors who bought you and enslaved you, we are their children. We are the new generation. Why don't you call us your brothers?

Malcolm: A man has to act like a brother before you can call him a brother. You made a very good point, really, that needs some clarification. If you are the son of a man who had a wealthy estate and you inherit your father's estate, you have to pay off the debts that your father incurred before he died. The only reason that the present generation of white Americans are in the position of economic strength that they are is because their fathers worked our fathers for over 400 years with no pay. For over 400 years we worked for nothing. We were sold from plantation to plantation like you sell a horse, or a cow, or a chicken, or a bushel of wheat. It was your fathers that did it to our fathers, and all of that money that piled up from the sale of my mother and my grandmother and my great-grandmother is what gives the present generation of American whites [the ability] to walk around the earth with their chest out; you know, like they have some kind of economic ingenuity. Your father isn't here to pay his debts. My father isn't here to collect. But I'm here to collect and you're here to pay.

Question 20: Malcolm X, whatever the official position of the governments that constitute the Organization of African Unity at the moment, one is certain that all

the African people, all the organizations and all progressive men whose role it is to understand your position, cannot but support your struggle. I would like to
ask you whether your recent tour in Africa has given
you reasons to hope that you are understood and supported?

Malcolm: Yes. I might point out that I went to Cairo,
Khartoum, Addis Ababa, Nairobi, Zanzibar (which is
a beautiful place), Dar es Salaam, Lagos, Accra, Mon-
rovia, Conakry, Algiers, on the African continent; and
then in the Middle East to Mecca, Kuwait, Beirut. I've
been travelling eighteen weeks. I'm going to New York
tomorrow and I have not gone into any African country and run into any closed minds or closed hearts or
closed doors. I encountered nothing but the spirit of
brotherhood and understanding and concern and I'm
greatly enthused over the tour that I made, and I know
the man back home is greatly concerned over the tour.
I hope that verifies your question.

Question 21: What I want to say is that you're right
in saying that the spotlight that you give on Africa is
very important from the psychological point of view,
but during the 400 years of deportation of the blacks
in America there was true militancy in the black people
because there were 156 revolts and there were famous
people like Sojourner Truth or Frederick Douglass. Do
you not think that it would be important for the new
black generation to know, from the historical point of
view, the militancy of Negroes in America?

Malcolm: Yes, it's important but it's even more important for us to be reestablished and connected to our
roots. Douglass was great. I would rather have been
taught about Toussaint L'Ouverture. We need to be
taught about people who fought, who bled for freedom
and made others bleed.

Question 22 (same questioner): The first guy that
was shot at the moment of the Independence War was
a Negro.

Malcolm: He wasn't shot for Negroes. He was shot
for America. I don't want to take away from Crispus

Attucks, but he was shot. He was a slave. His people were slaves.

Question 23 (same questioner): He was a slave perhaps, but not on his knees — on his feet.

Malcolm: Sir, you can take a dog — a big vicious dog — and sic him on somebody else and he's fearless. I'd like to give you an example. No matter how fearless a dog is, you catch him out on the street, stamp your foot; he'll run because you're only threatening him. His master has never trained him how to defend himself; but that same dog, if you walk through the master's gate, will growl and bite. Why will he growl and bite over there and not growl and bite over here? Over here he's growling and biting for the defense of his master and the benefit of his master, but when his own interests are threatened he has no growl. Not only Crispus Attucks, but many of us in America have died defending America. We defend our master. We're the most violent soldiers America has when she sends us to Korea or to the South Pacific or to Saigon, but when our mothers and our own property are being attacked we're nonviolent. Crispus Attucks laid down his life for America, but would he have laid down his life to stop the white man in America from enslaving black people?

So when you select heroes about which black children ought to be taught, let them be black heroes who have died fighting for the benefit of black people. We never were taught about Christophe or Dessalines. It was the slave revolt in Haiti when slaves, black slaves, had the soldiers of Napoleon tied down and forced him to sell one half of the American continent to the Americans. They don't teach us that. This is the kind of history we want to learn.

Question 24 (same questioner): What was the name of that man who worked for the underground? A great hero, a Negro?

Malcolm: Okay. He's okay but we want . . . It doesn't take away from him but we're more interested in what Toussaint did than how he did it, because he set up the only black republic in the Western Hemisphere. The only place where a black man sits in the top chair is in Haiti and that's because they did it through revolution. In no country has the black man ever come to the top — not even in your so-called socialist, Marxist, and other type societies have they ever had a black man on top.

[*Very lengthy speech in French from somebody in the audience.*]

Malcolm: I would like to thank all of you who have been so patient this evening and have remained here for so long. I hope that no one will get the impression that because I raise my voice from time to time that it is out of disrespect. It's not. It's just that it's the only way I can emphasize how deplorable the situation, which has continued so long, really is. And one of the best ways you can help us in the States is to watch the problem very closely. And when they grab us and arrest us, let them know, well, that they shouldn't have done it.

AN EXCHANGE

ON CASUALTIES

8 IN THE CONGO

Malcolm X returned from abroad on November 24, 1964, and participated in a discussion about the civil war in the Congo on the Barry Gray Show broadcast over Station WMCA in New York on November 28.

The other panelists were Dr. Hugh H. Smythe, then of Brooklyn College; Dr. Sanford Griffith, then of the New School for Social Research and New York University; and Dr. James H. Robinson of the Church of the Master in Harlem and the head of Operation Crossroads Africa.

The following excerpts, which include part of Malcolm's opening remarks and a subsequent exchange with Dr. Griffith, are printed here for the first time.

Malcolm X: I was thinking about what Dr. Griffith said concerning Belgium's benevolent rule of the Congo and the degree to which they were able to exercise control and keep the casualties at a minimum. I was reading a book today by Mark Twain called *King Leopold's*

127

Soliloquy, about Belgium. And it stated in there that
when Belgium took over, the population of the Congo
was something like 30 million and they reduced it to
15 million. If these aren't casualties, I don't know what
casualties are.

But while the Belgians were butchering the Congolese
you'll find that the historians haven't recorded where
there was all this concern, at that time, over the loss
of human lives, as long as they were black lives. It
seems that there wasn't as much value placed upon
them as was placed upon the handful of white hostages
whose lives were threatened here earlier in the week. . . .

I think too much time is spent by newspapers, commentators, and some of these so-called scientists who are
supposed to be authorities trying to prove that the Congolese are savage, that they are not fully developed, that
they are not able to govern themselves. Most of the
things that we've seen in print usually are designed toward that end, and this is not done actually to prove
that they are savage as much as it is done to justify
what the Western powers are doing in the Congo, or
the presence of the Western powers in the Congo, and
primarily the presence of the United States.

The basic cause of most of the trouble in the Congo
right now is the intervention of outsiders — the fighting
that is going on over the mineral wealth of the Congo
and over the strategic position that the Congo represents
on the African continent. And in order to justify it, they
are doing it at the expense of the Congolese, by trying
to make it appear that the people are savages. And I
think, as one of the gentlemen mentioned earlier, if there
are savages in the Congo then there are worse savages
in Mississippi, Alabama, and New York City, and probably some in Washington, D. C., too.

Dr. Sanford Griffith: It seems to me that there is a
confusion of degree here that is unfortunate. In the first
place, Malcolm X's statement, his figures on the Belgian
history of the Congo, is grossly distorted. I would point
out that there were two phases of Belgian occupation of
the Congo. The first was the period of King Leopold's
rule, which ran from the middle eighties till about 1912,

and a second period since then, where the Belgian government took over from King Leopold and actually made a serious attempt, with considerable success, of introducing a type of colonial government which had many qualities to be admired rather than deplored.

The figures of casualties in the Congo, the purported killings by the Belgians — I would say two things. In the first place, the precolonial era, the slave centuries, exacted a terrific toll in the Congo and the casualties were tremendous. That is a crime which not only the Europeans and Americans but also the Africans themselves must share the responsibility for. The period after the Belgian government took over the Congo, from 1908-1912 on, was a period of high administrative development, of performance by a vast number of conscientious and efficient Belgian public servants.

The criticism that can be made of the Belgian regime in the Congo from the 1912 period on is a criticism of lack of understanding on the part of the Belgians that the Congolese people should be expected to participate and should reasonably look toward independence at not some highly remote period, did not educate, did not give the Congolese an opportunity to develop the talents, and they have just as much natural talent as any other people, to develop the talents which would have permitted them to operate successfully this vast country.

Now that is an aspect of the situation which should not be overlooked. And I would point out that the Belgian administration of the Congo still in many respects gives an example of fine administration which the Congolese themselves and other people can also benefit from.

Malcolm: Please, just one little short one. Dr. Griffith, you say I exaggerated the number of deaths. I said he reduced it from 30 million to 15 million. How many million did he —

Griffith: This was not, look, this was not —

Malcolm: If I say that there were 15 million casualties and I am exaggerating it, tell me how many there were?

Griffith: In the first place, may I say this?

Malcolm: Sir, will you tell me how many million casualties there were?

Griffith: Well, are you going to give me a chance to answer you? In the first place, we have no statistics. We use round figures. We don't even know within—

Malcolm: Just give me some round figures.

Griffith: Pardon me, we don't even know the number of slaves that were taken out of Africa over the whole period.

Malcolm: Give me an estimate.

Griffith: The number varies between 10 and 20 million over a period of a couple of hundred years. As far as the Congo is concerned, let me say this. King Leopold—

Malcolm: Give me an estimate, sir.

Griffith: I would say that probably through the concessionaires who exploited the natives into collecting rubber, there were undoubtedly many thousand casualties, but certainly not a hundred thousand and certainly not fifty thousand.

Malcolm: I didn't say, I said that the Mark Twain book pointed out—

Griffith: Mark Twain is not a historian.

Malcolm: Some of these that you now see calling themselves historians are not historians. Mark Twain points out that the population was reduced from 30 million to 15 million by this man Leopold. You say that I am exaggerating. How many million was it?

Griffith: There was no million. Look, Leopold's rubber gatherers exterminated a lot of natives who didn't bring in their quotas of rubber.

Malcolm: How did he exterminate them—

Griffith: Pardon me, it was a shocking thing to have happened, but it does not represent anything like the mass murders that you're describing.

Barry Gray: I think we are going to get lost in past history rather than the present events which are occupying the front pages of the headlines. I would agree that we have to know something of the background in order to address ourselves to the present, but I am afraid that the entire program might be devoted to King Leopold instead of the present-day Congo.

Malcolm: One of the gentlemen said earlier, I think

it was Dr. Robinson, that he saw a seething, what was that, some very strong feelings that were hostile, down beneath the surface, in these people. And I think the only way a person can be justified in condemning the Congolese the way that the press is in the process of condemning them right now, they would have to go back in history to find out what it is that made these people act as they do towards these Europeans.

Gray: Malcolm, I don't hear anyone asking this question, so I must; I am curious. I can understand the normal reaction and rage at oppressors when the oppressed get an opportunity to act equally or with superior force. I don't understand, though, how that rage can be effectively shown against nuns, missionaries, etc. Now that's in the news.

Malcolm: Certainly it is in the news. But I think it was just as much in the news when the people who were doing the oppressing were cutting off the breasts of black women when they didn't produce their rubber quota; cutting off their hands, cutting off their feet. This is historic fact. And when you start talking about what the Congolese are doing in retaliation today, they have pictures that are historic fact, that Leopold made it mandatory that when a black man didn't produce a certain quota of rubber, his hand was cut off, his foot was cut off, a black woman's breast was cut off. This is what took place in the Congo. And it took place for a long time.

It's easy to gloss all that over today and make it look like the Belgians went in there with some kind of benevolent intent. But the Congolese are just as humane, just as human, and just as intelligent as anybody else on this planet. And when they reflect this animosity and hostility I think anyone who goes over there and examines the facts will find out they're justified. In fact, I think that they showed remarkable restraint, given the fact that the paratroopers were able to rescue somebody.

Talking to reporters at Kennedy International Airport upon his return from Africa, November 24, 1964. In the background are Malcolm's wife and children.

Photo by Robert Parent

THE HOMECOMING
9 RALLY OF THE OAAU

Malcolm X gave the following speech at the Audubon Ballroom on November 29, 1964, at the first rally held by the OAAU after his extended visit to Africa and the Mideast. It is printed here for the first time.

Salaam Alaikum, all my brothers and sisters. Well, I hardly know how to get started, but I can let you know in advance that we're not going to keep you here tonight very long. I first have to make a confession — I almost didn't get here tonight; something came up, a situation developed where we were going to almost have to postpone our little brief talk until next Sunday. But thanks to the one that created the universe — some call him God; some call him a whole lot of things; I call him Allah — I'm thankful to be able to be here.

Now, brothers and sisters, all I would like to do tonight, and I beg your forgiveness, is to give you a brief sketch or outline on some experiences that I've

had during the past eighteen weeks. It's certainly good
to be back, although I don't know how a black man
can leave a black continent and come back to a white
continent and say it's good to be back. I would like
to give a brief sketch to you concerning some of the
experiences that I've had, some of the things I've seen,
some of the things I've heard, so that you can evaluate
them with your own mind.

The reason that it has to be brief is that I have to
leave the country again this week. I'll be back next
Sunday, but I'm involved in a debate at Oxford University in England, outside of London, on Thursday.
I have to go there for that, and then come back here
for a rally which we're going to have next Sunday night,
at which time we are going to try and get some experts to come and give us an outline of exactly what
has taken place in the Congo, so that the black people
in Harlem won't have to be involved in a situation
where we'll be sitting on the log, wondering what's
going on. I think that you and I should realize that
the time has come for us to let the world know that
we're not only interested in some kind of integrated
situation in the United States, but we're interested in
taking our place on the world stage, and we're interested in anything that involves black people anywhere
on this earth.

It would be a crime for you and me to be in a city
that has more black people in it than any other city
on this earth, New York City, and be silent in the face
of the criminal action of the United States government
in conjunction with Belgium in the Congo. I mean criminal, criminal action that this government has involved
itself in. Lyndon B. Johnson — he said it today, he's to
blame. He doesn't have to say it; we know he's to blame
before he said it. He waited until the people had voted
for him and he got in, and things got cut and dried.
Then he got in cahoots with Belgium — one of the worst
racist governments that has ever existed on the face
of the earth, Belgium. This government, in conjunction
with that government, is dropping paratroopers in the

Congo under the pretext that it's some kind of human-
itarian operation.

So next Sunday night we are going to try and get
some of our African brothers and some of our Afro-
American brothers who are well versed in the facts concerning the history of the Congo [to tell] how the white
man happend to be over there in the first place, why
he is over there still and finds it so difficult to leave,
and most important of all, what are the factors behind
the deep-rooted hostility that seems to lie in the hearts
of our Congolese brothers toward them. We want to
know if our brothers are savage, as they keep imply-
ing, or are they justified in the feelings that they've been
displaying toward these people who are over there in
their land, not by their invitation?

I don't want to get on that, but this is what we want
next Sunday night, and we're going to try and get some
help in outlining the incidents that led up to the present
situation in the Congo today. But never believe what
you read in the newspapers -- they're not going to tell
you the truth. The truth isn't in them. Not when it comes
to the Congo; they can't tell the truth. I was on the
radio with a man the other night, and he had the nerve
to tell on the air about some Congolese atrocities, and
the benevolence of the Belgian government, and how
[Belgian] atrocities never took place. I didn't believe
that a white man, so intelligent, would have so much
nerve in 1964. I could see him taking that stand in
1924, or even 1944, or maybe 1954, but not 1964.

So, brothers and sisters, when I left here on the 9th
of July, it was primarily because I had just been successful in starting a new religious organization which
many of you have heard about, the Muslim Mosque,
Inc., and we had also just been successful in organizing
a new nonreligious organization, the Organization of
Afro-American Unity. One of the main reasons for un-
dertaking the journey was to lay a foundation. It is
impossible for any black group in America to become
involved in any kind of religion that doesn't have roots
directly connected with some source in the East. And

it is impossible for any black group in America to become involved in any kind of political organization that doesn't have some roots directly connected with our roots on the African continent.

You waste your time involving yourself in any kind of organization that is not directly connected with our brothers and sisters on the African continent. Can I prove it? Yes. There was a time in this country when they used to use the expression about Chinese, "He doesn't have a Chinaman's chance." Remember when they used to say that about the Chinese? You don't hear them saying that nowadays. Because the Chinaman has more chance now than they do. And what makes the cheese so binding is he has the same things they have, and will use it faster than they will.

It was not until China became independent and strong that Chinese people all over the world became respected. They never became respected by sitting-in, begging-in, praying-in, kneeling-in, or crawling-in. They became respected only when China as a nation became independent and strong. And then they had something behind them, they had someone behind them. Once China became independent and strong and feared, then wherever you saw a Chinaman, he was independent, he was strong, he was feared and he was respected.

It's the same way with you and me. They can pass every kind of bill imaginable in Washington, D. C., and you and I will never be respected, because we have nothing behind us. The law is not behind us. Washington, D. C., is not behind us. Nor are the Congress, the Senate, and the President behind us. We haven't got anything in this country behind you and me. You and I have to get our people behind us, our people in our own motherland and fatherland. Just as a strong China has produced a respected Chinaman, a strong Africa will produce a respected black man anywhere that black man goes on this earth. It's only with a strong Africa, an independent Africa and a respected Africa that wherever those of African origin or African heritage or African likeness go, they will be respected.

But as long as Africa is not respected, it doesn't make

any difference if you're a doctor or lawyer — why, they'll bounce your head like a knot on a log, no matter where you go. Can I prove it? Yes. While I was in Africa, this young Negro educator in Georgia — he wasn't ragged, he wasn't uncouth, he wasn't uncivilized; he was an educator, he was as uppity and dicty as they were — and they still shot him. Why? Because he had nothing behind him. His education couldn't save him, his degrees couldn't save him, his profession couldn't save him. No, because he didn't have anything behind him. The government wasn't behind him. But had Africa been a strong, independent entity that was respected and recognized by every other power on this earth, then the brother, who reflected all the characteristics of an African, whether he liked it or not, would have been respected by even the Klan and other people down there who are supposed to be so ignorant and don't respect the rights of our people.

So I say that we must have a strong Africa, and one of my reasons for going to Africa was because I know this. You waste your time in this country, in any kind of strategy that you use, if you're not in direct contact with your brother on the African continent who has his independence. He has problems, but he still has his independence, and in that independence he has a voice; in that voice there is strength. And when you and I link our struggle up with his struggle, so that his struggle backs our struggle, you'll find that this man over here will pay a little more attention. You can sit on his doorstep all day long nonviolently; he'll pay you some attention, but not the kind you want.

So, brothers and sisters, about the past 18 weeks: First I was in Cairo, in Egypt, which is Africa, for two months. Cairo is a very interesting city, in that you can find more headquarters there for organizations involved in freedom struggles for Asians, Africans, and Latin Americans perhaps than in any other city on earth at this time. It's not an accident that so many summit conferences have taken place there. It's just a revolutionary city.

And all thinking people today who have been oppressed are revolutionary. Any time you find somebody today who's afraid of the word "revolution," get him on out of your way. He's living in the wrong era. He's behind the times. He hasn't awakened yet. This is the era of revolution.

Now I must just take time to clarify what I mean before some of these pencil-scratchers misquote me, which they're going to do anyway. You notice two years ago the American press was calling your and my struggle a revolution — "Negro revolution, Negro revolution." Now, they didn't mind calling it that, and they didn't mind you referring to it as that, because they knew that what was happening was no revolution. But when you start using the word "revolution" in its real sense, then they get shaky. They start classifying you as a fanatic, or something subversive or seditious, or other than a law-abiding person. But today we're living in an era of revolution, which means an era of change, when people who are being oppressed want a change. And they don't want a gradual change. They don't want the change that comes year by year, or week by week, or month by month. They want a change right now.

Cairo is one of the cities on this earth that has the headquarters for more revolutionary movements, I imagine, than any other city. By the way, when I got there, as you know, they were having the African summit conference. All of our brothers were over there, getting together, discussing the problems of the world. It was a beautiful sight, especially when you live in a country where you and I don't have any chance to discuss anything but an integrated cup of coffee, or how to integrate some toilet in Mississippi. When you go and find independent African nations, headed by their leaders, their heads of state, sitting down and discussing problems of the world, the economic, political, and social problems of the world, why, it makes you feel good, it makes you get a new lease on life.

When I got there, there was a great deal of pressure already being put on various segments of the African

community to not open any doors, and these pressures
were being put down by *this* government. I started not
to say this government, but I'm going to tell the truth
the way it is, let the chips fall where they may.

They had their men over there running around like
mad with their money, trying to make it impossible for
any American Negro to be included in any way in any
conference dealing with Africans, or dealing with international affairs. They try to give the impression over
there that you and I aren't interested in international
affairs, that you and I are interested only in integrating
Mississippi. This is the image that is very skillfully spread
abroad of the American Negro, that you and I cannot
see beyond the shores of America — that our minds and
our thoughts and our desires and our hopes are limited
to everything right here.

Naturally, any African who would believe this is
shocked when he sees an Afro-American coming to an
international conference, especially a conference that's
composed just of independent African states. Some of
them this government has tried to give the impression
over there that you and I don't even identify with Africa.
And some of them get shocked when they see you and
me turning in their direction.

I'm telling you, they've done a vicious job. This thing
they call the USIS, the United States Information Service,
is one of the most vicious organs that has ever been
put together and sent anywhere by any country. It will
make that propaganda machine that Goebbels had, under
Hitler, look like child's play.

Why, in every African country the USIS window has
pictures in it, showing the passage of the civil rights
bill to make it look like the problems of every Negro
over here have been solved. Go in any African country,
and you know before you get there what's going to be
in the window. They use the passage of the civil rights
bill to make it appear that Negroes aren't being lynched
any more, that Negroes' voting rights aren't being tram-
pled upon any more, that police aren't busting Negroes'
heads with clubs any more, nor are they using dogs

and violence and water hoses to wash us down the drain. They make it appear that the civil rights bill created a paradise in the United States for the 22 million Negroes. This is the thing they call USIS. It does a very bad job of creating the wrong image and giving the wrong impression.

To show you how vicious they are — I'm within my rights to attack it; actually I'm not attacking it, I'm only analyzing it. On the 4th of November, the date that the election was over, the USIS circulated a document on me throughout the African continent — knocking me, you know. Here I am, just a little old poor so-called Negro from Harlem, and they're going to waste all their paper trying to tell Africans, "Don't listen to what that man says, because he doesn't represent anything, and doesn't represent anybody, and has always been discredited." That's your USIS. I say a prayer for them.

I want to say this too, in passing, for the benefit of our Muslim brothers and sisters who might be here from some of the Muslim countries, and might get a bit nervous over what I'm saying, and the way I'm saying it. This is not a religious meeting. When I come to a meeting sponsored by the OAAU, which is the Organization of Afro-American Unity, I put my religion in this pocket right here, and keep it here. And when I talk like this, it doesn't mean I'm less religious, it means I'm more religious. I believe in a religion that believes in freedom. Any time I have to accept a religion that won't let me fight a battle for my people, I say to hell with that religion. That's why I am a Muslim, because it's a religion that teaches you an eye for an eye and a tooth for a tooth. It teaches you to respect everybody, and treat everybody right. But it also teaches you if someone steps on your toe, chop off their foot. And I carry my religious axe with me all the time.

You know they have freedom movements on the African continent. There are many liberation movements; there are movements of Africans from South Africa, from Mozambique, from South-West Africa, Bechuanaland, Swaziland, Angola. In every country, in every area on the African continent that has not tossed aside the shackles of colonialism, they have developed a liberation movement, and the purpose of these liberation movements is to throw aside the oppressor.

After the summit conference, the most respected groups were these freedom fighters. The heads of the various liberation movements from the different parts of the African continent were all housed on a ship that was anchored in the Nile River — a ship called the Isis. They were placed there so that they could all be together, and discuss the problems that they had in common. At the same time it was excellent for security purposes, because you can't get on a boat so easily.

I was blessed with the opportunity to live on that boat with the leaders of the liberation movements, because I represented an Afro-American liberation movement — Afro-American freedom fighters. And all of us were on there together. It gave me an opportunity to study, to listen and study the type of people involved in the struggle — their thinking, their objectives, their aims and their methods. It opened my eyes to many things. And I think I was able to steal a few ideas that they used, and tactics and strategy, that will be most effective in your and my freedom struggle here in this country.

Some of them were nonviolent — I didn't listen too long to any of those. And others really want freedom. When a person places a proper value on freedom, there is nothing under the sun that he will not do to acquire that freedom. Whenever you hear a man saying he wants freedom, but in the next breath he is going to tell you what he won't do to get it, or what he doesn't believe in doing in order to get it, he doesn't believe in freedom. A man who believes in freedom will do anything under the sun to acquire or achieve his freedom, and he will do anything under the sun to preserve his freedom. And the only reason you and I here in America don't yet have freedom is we haven't yet matured to that stage where we can see this is the real price, or the real attitude, or the real approach that one must make.

I was, as I said, in Egypt, the United Arab Republic,

for two months, and then left and went to Mecca, where
I was for about a week; I was in Saudi Arabia for
about a week, and Mecca a couple of days. I left there
and went to Kuwait, where all the oil is, on the Persian
Gulf, and from there to Beirut in Lebanon. After spend-
ing two months there, in the Middle East, then I went
on into other parts of Africa, the first stop being Khartoum where, since then, they've had a whole lot of
trouble—which they should have had. Now everything
is all settled; they had a revolution, and got people
that didn't belong in power out of power—that's how
you do it. And that's what they did, the students.

The students all over the world are the ones who bring
about a change; old people don't bring about a change.
I mean I'm not saying this against anybody that's old—
because if you're ready for some action you're not old,
I don't care how old you are. But if you're not ready
for some action, I don't care how young you are, you're
old. As long as you want some action, you're young.
But any time you begin to sit on the fence, and your
toes start shaking because you're afraid too much action is going down, then you're too old; you need to
get on out of the way. Some of us get too old while
we're still in our teens.

So, I went through Khartoum to Addis Ababa, Ethiopia,
which is a wonderful country. It has its problems, and
it's still a wonderful country. Some of the most beautiful
people I've seen are in Ethiopia, and most intelligent
and most dignified, right there in Ethiopia. You hear
all kinds of propaganda about Ethiopia. But any time
a person tries to tell you, as they've told you and me,
that Ethiopians don't think they're the same as we are,
that's some of that man's manufacturing. He made that
up.   You know who I mean when I say "that man."
They're just as friendly toward us as anybody else is.

I was there for about a week, and went on into Kenya,
a place which really knocked me out. If ever I saw any
Africans who looked like they have the potential for
explosion, it's our good Kikuyu brothers in Kenya.
I was discussing my opinion of the people of Kenya,

especially in Nairobi, with some friends while I was there, and I told them that I was looking at the faces of these people, and they looked like they can explode. And they do; they look like they can explode, more so than any place I went on the continent. You can just see, right in their faces, energy. Now if you channel it in the right direction, it goes in the right direction; if you let it go in the wrong direction, it goes in the wrong direction — but they've got the energy, that's the most important thing.

And as proof that they can explode, they exploded the other day. When the United States, with her criminal action in the Congo — and that's what it is, criminal action in the Congo — they marched on the embassy there in Nairobi, tore it up. And that shows you what the Africans feel. They don't like to see anybody exploiting another African or oppressing another African; they stick together, and you and I can learn that's what we're supposed to do. When something happens in Mississippi, we don't have to go to Mississippi — they've got some people that look just like those in Mississippi, right here.

My contention is, those up here are just as much responsible for what's happening down there as those down there. And when you and I let them know that we hold all of them responsible, then all of them will start acting right. They'll keep those others in line. But as long as you and I make them think they can pass the buck, then they will be passing the buck, they'll be telling us, you know, "Mississippi," and they're doing the same thing right here.

So, when I left Kenya, I went to Zanzibar and Tanganyika; now it's called Tanzania. And I never went anywhere that has pleased me more than that place. It's beautiful — all of Africa is beautiful — but in Tanganyika, it's a very beautiful place. It's hot, it's like Miami, Miami is hot, and if these people pay as much money as they do to live in Miami, why, you know, the entire African continent where I went is just like Miami Beach. And they're always telling you and me, you know, how difficult a time we would have trying to adjust if we went over there. I'm telling you, if you want to integrate, go to Africa. There are more white people over there than there are over here. That's where they all are. They're over there living like kings, basking in the sun.

When I left Tanganyika, I went back to Kenya, and from Kenya back to Ethiopia, and from Ethiopia to Nigeria, which is another beautiful land, but in West Africa. I was there for several days, and then went to Ghana, and from Ghana to Liberia, and Liberia to Conakry, Guinea, a most beautiful country—it's got one of the best presidents on the African continent—and then from there to Algiers, Algeria.

In fact, I missed my plane. I was supposed to go directly from Conakry via Lomako to Algiers by Aeroflot, and I missed it, not through my own doing. The plane company didn't give me the right information. They said that the plane left at 11:55. I got to the airport at 11 o'clock, and they told me it had left at 8 o'clock that morning. I talked to them in four languages, so on Friday the 13th they put me on a plane to get me to Algiers. To show you what a small world this is, I had breakfast in Conakry on Friday the 13th, I had lunch in Dakar in Senegal, and dinner that evening in Geneva, I went to bed that night in Paris, and was in Algiers the next morning at 10 o'clock. When the man made these airplanes for you and me, he made them so we could get around and let our brothers know what's happening.

So, brothers and sisters, I tell you that to let you know that in all of the traveling that I did, in the Middle East and in Africa, everywhere I went, I found nothing but open minds, I found nothing but open hearts, and I found nothing but open doors. Our people love us; all they want to know is, do we love them?

While I was traveling, I had an opportunity to speak with President Nasser when I was in Egypt. I also had an opportunity to speak with President Nyerere for three hours while I was in Dar es Salaam; he's a most intelligent man, and alert, and knows what's going on. Also, when I was in Nigeria, I had a chance to speak with President Azikiwe in Lagos. And President Nkrumah, who *stays* up to date; he can tell you so much about what's happening in Harlem you think he's out there on the corner with you. You can quickly see why this man doesn't like him — he's hip to them, brothers.

Then I spent three days at the oceanside home of President Sékou Touré in Conakry, and I found him to be a man who lives by keeping himself well informed. He's very much concerned with the problems and the plight of our people in this country, and has excellent advice, too, to give toward solving it. When I was in Tanganyika, I was fortunate enough to be able to ride on the same plane with Prime Minister Jomo Kenyatta and Prime Minister Dr. Milton Obote, when they were up through Uganda, when they were going from Dar es Salaam to Zanzibar, back to Kenya. I had my movie camera, and I had a chance while we were in Zanzibar to film Kenyatta when he was involved in a press conference, which was beautiful. I'll show those films here some time within the next two or three weeks.

They show the young brothers in Zanzibar. When you see those brothers there in Zanzibar you know why this man over here is worried. Those brothers have got a whole lot on the ball, brothers, and they don't play. In fact, not many Americans make it to Zanzibar. They don't go for Americans too much over there. This doesn't mean they're anti-American. But they know them.

My main theme, while I was traveling with our brothers abroad, on the African continent, was to try and impress upon them that 22 million of our people here in America consider ourselves inseparably linked with them, that our origin is the same and our destiny is the same, and that we have been kept apart now for too long.

This doesn't mean that we're getting ready to pack up our bags and take a boat back to Africa. This was not the impression that I was trying to give, because this is not true. You don't find any large number of our people packing up their bags going back to Africa.

That's not necessary. But what is necessary is that we
have to go back mentally, we have to go back culturally,
we have to go back spiritually, and philosophically,
and psychologically.

And when we go back in that sense, then this spiritual bond that is created makes us inseparable, and they
can see that our problem is their problem, and their
problem is our problem. Our problem is not solved
until theirs is solved, theirs is not solved until ours is
solved. And when we can develop that kind of relationship, then it means that we will help them solve their
problems, and we want them to help us solve our problems. And by both of us working together, we'll get
a solution to that problem. We will only get that problem solved by working together.

This was the essence of every discussion—that the
problems are one, that the destiny is the same, the origin
is the same. Even the experiences are the same; they catch
hell, we catch hell. And no matter how much independence they've got, on that land, on the mother continent,
if we don't have it over here, and don't have respect
over here, when they come over here they are mistaken
for one of us and they are disrespected too. So in order
[for them] to be respected, we must be respected.

And I say, brothers and sisters, they're beginning
to see this. They're beginning to see that the problems
are one. They are interested in our problems, but they
were shocked to learn that we were also interested in
their problems. And if I would have any advice to give
to our people here in the Western Hemisphere, I would
say that it has been almost criminal on our part, all
the organizations that we have, for us not to have tried
to make some kind of direct contact, direct communica-
tion, with our brothers on the African continent before.

We should never let the white man represent us to
them, and we should never let him represent them to
us. It is our job today to represent ourselves, as they
are representing themselves. We don't need someone else
representing us. We don't want anybody to tell somebody how we think. We will let the world know how we

think. We don't want any handkerchief-head set up by
the State Department as a spokesman for us, telling
the world how we think; we want the world to know
how we think. We want the world to know we don't like
what Sam is doing in the Congo to our brothers and
sisters.

I must say this, in brief. I was talking to a brother
from the Congo, who was very angry. I was in Tanganyika, he had just come from Leopoldville, and he
was very angry because he told me that out of all of
the paratroopers, or eighty paratroopers—you'll have
to stop handing me these things while I'm up here; it's
getting like Grand Central Station, you send my mind
somewhere else. He was telling me that he was very
angry at American Negroes. And he was talking about
us, you know, like a dog. Not me, because he knows
what I represent. The best thing the white man ever did
for me was to make me look like a monster all over
the world. Because I can go any place on the African
continent and our African brothers know where I stand.

He was angry because he said that most of the paratroopers, the American soldiers that were guarding these
transports that Tshombe was using, were American
Negroes; that they put American soldiers in there. I
never had a chance to check it out. Normally I wouldn't
stand up in a public meeting and say it, but when I
first heard it, and I heard it from an Afro-American
who works over there, I went to track this brother from
the Congo down. He's a very intelligent fellow, and he
said "yes," and he was hot, you know. And so I sat
down to let him know that all of us don't think like
that. That they had to go all over the United States
with a microscope and find that many Negroes dumb
enough to let themselves be sent to the Congo—imagine,
a Negro that lets himself be sent to the Congo!—in a
uniform, against people who look just like he does. Why,
he should be shot. So I let him know that that wasn't
us, that was somebody else.

Also, brothers and sisters, you know Tshombe. You've
heard of him. From what I understand, Tshombe arrives

in the United States on Tuesday. He's got a whole lot
of nerve. The best thing they did for him in Cairo was
when they locked him up. That protected him. Because
Tshombe can't go to any country where there are true
black men, *true* black men, and walk the street in safety.
This is the worst African that was ever born. The worst
African that was ever born. This is the man who in
cold blood, cold blood, committed an international
crime — murdered Patrice Lumumba, murdered him in
cold blood. The world knows that Tshombe murdered
LΛumumba. And now he's a bed partner for Lyndon B. Johnson. Yes, a bed partner. They're sleeping
together, they're sleeping together. When I say sleeping
together, I don't mean that literally. But beyond that
they're in the same bed. Johnson is paying the salaries,
paying the government, propping up Tshombe'sʹ government, this murderer. It is the Lyndon B. Johnson administration, the man you voted for — you were insane,
out of your mind, out of your head, to vote for a man
like that; drunk. But I don't blame you, you just were
tricked. I told you a fox will always get business.

So Tshombe arrives here on Tuesday. And many of
our brothers that belong to the African student associa-
tion plan to give him a welcome. Shucks, I have a religion that believes in hospitality. Everybody should be
welcome — according to their just desserts. So the brother
that's involved in this, I think Sidi Ali — where is he?
Sidi Ali, come and give this announcement. This is our
brother, Sidi Ali of Ghana.

[*Sidi Ali, secretary of the New York chapter of the Pan-
African Student Union, speaks about the situation in the
Congo and invites the audience to participate in the
demonstration planned against Tshombe at the United
Nations. Malcolm continues:*]

Brothers and sisters, I have some quick announcements.
Next week the Audubon is not available, so our next
meeting will be on the 13th, which will be two weeks from
tonight. At that time the topic will be "The Congo Crisis."
I imagine the crisis won't be over. Because it's of such
nature that they're in there now and they can't come

out with clean hands. It's almost impossible for them to pull out. They went in there and killed people; now, when they pull back out, what do you think will happen? They can't get out of it like that.

One thing you must always bear in mind, as our brother pointed out, these young brothers that are in the Stanleyville area, Oriental Province, are not rebels, as the press continues to refer to them. They call themselves Simbas, which means lions, you know, meaning they've got it. They're freedom fighters, and your and my heart should be with theirs. They are men, they are men, the proof of which is they are dying to get their freedom. They're killing too, but so what? They've been killed themselves — all they do is believe in equality. What's good for the goose is good for the goose.

Also, always bear in mind, that the only Congolese soldiers that are winning any battles, or that have won any battles, have been those brothers who are the freedom fighters. The Congolese soldiers that fight for Tshombe don't win battles. They were giving up in the face of the freedom fighters. They were giving up the entire Congo. They were evacuating the place and the United States got desperate. That's why they went and got Tshombe, went all the way up in Spain, where Tshombe had retired, had given up, was living the life, and they talked him into going back to the Congo and becoming the premier.

As soon as they got him back into position as premier, the first thing he did was bring in some white mercenaries, murderers — because that's what a mercenary means, it means a hired killer. And this government, the United States government, supplies the salaries for these hired killers from your tax dollars. Every time you pay your taxes you are paying the salary for those white blue-eyed murderers there in the Congo who are killing the Congolese. There's nobody in the State Department can deny it.

In fact, I read in the paper today where Lyndon B. Johnson said he'd take full responsibility. He should take full responsibility. He's pulling the same kind of an act over there in the Congo that they've been pulling in Texas on you and me for the past two or three hundred years. That's a Texas act. You know what kind of act goes on in Texas. But they can't win because the only way Tshombe can remain premier is with help from the outside. He must get white help. So, as long as Tshombe remains the premier of the Congo, it means the white man is going to have to continue sending white soldiers in there to rescue him. And he'll lose every white soldier he has, he'll lose them in there.

So, those brothers know what they're doing—in fact, what you and I need to do. What you and I need to do. Many of us are vets, we've had all kind of experience. You've seen all kinds of action, haven't you? But you've never seen any action for yourself, and you've never seen any action for anybody who is of your own kind. Many of you are unemployed. We might put on a drive right here in Harlem to raise up some black mercenaries to take over there to show them what to do.

You see, there's some kind of cultural, psychological block in the minds of our brothers there, or these white mercenaries wouldn't have the advantage. All they have is the psychological advantage. They wouldn't have that on you and me. You and I don't have that block, we don't have that cultural block because they destroyed our culture. We can think just like they think now. We can do the same thing they can do. You just give me ten black ones and we'll eat up fifty of those white ones. Eat them up.

And there's nothing wrong with that. Why? Because this government, this same government has recruited what they call "anti-Castro Cubans." Which means they're American. And this government sends them over there to bomb the Congolese. But they're afraid to say that they're American pilots, so they say they're anti-Castro Cuban pilots. Okay, we've got black people who can fly planes—we've been flying them for the man. Instead of you sitting around here driving a bus, remember how you used to fly a plane for him, get on over there

and get with it on the right side. If they can send white
ones against black ones, we can recruit and send black
ones against white ones. I frankly believe that it would
be most exciting. I know a whole lot of Afro-Americans
would go for free—would go for fun. We don't need
any money, we just want to get even.

Now, I'm going to tell you what they're going to do,
because I know them. In the paper tomorrow you're
going to read that a whole lot of frantic, you know,
statements were made. As long as there are white people
going over there shooting black people, nothing is said—
they glorify them. But when you and I start talking like
we want to do the same thing to some of them, then
we're *fanatics*, we're *bloodthirsty*. But I think then the
white man should know one thing—when I say white
man, I'm not saying all of you, whatever you are, because some of you might be all right. And whichever
one of you acts all right with me, you're all right with
me, as long as you act all right. But if you don't act
all right, you're not all right. All you've got to do to
be all right with me is act all right. But don't come
thinking you're all right just because you're white.

I think that that point has to be made because if you
don't clarify it, they go out of here saying you're a racist,
that you're against all white people. We're not against
all white people. We're against all those that aren't right,
all of them that aren't right.

We purposely aren't going to have any question and
answer period tonight. I don't think we need one. But
we are going to take up a collection because we pay for
this hall and we won't be able to get back here two weeks
from now unless we pay for it. And when I say *we*
pay for it, you know, *we*. Just let me take five minutes
right now real quick before I forget while the brothers
are coming to take up a collection.

And again, as soon as you start taking up a collection, you'll read in the papers tomorrow morning: "what
they did—they took up a collection." They write like
they're out of their mind. They always are intelligent
until they come around us. When you read what they

write someplace else, they write intelligently. But when
we let them in here and let them write, then they write
things that aren't even of interest. [Shouts from the audience.] You say, "Why let them in?" Sometime I'll tell
you why I let them in. But if you don't want them in
here, then keep them out.

[*During the collection, Malcolm makes further announcements. He reports the arrival of an African Muslim teacher from Mecca and tells when and where he will be speaking. To offset any feeling of religious favoritism, he offers
"to make an announcement for (any) church you belong
to, church or synagogue." He promises an effort will
be made to get scholars and experts from the United
Nations to speak at the next rally, "so we won't have
to go by what we read in the newspapers." Then he continues:*]

I think our brother, Sidi Ali, did a wonderful job in
destroying that myth about cannibalism. The man is
always trying to make it look like our people are can-
nibals. The only cannibal I've ever seen, the only persons I've ever seen who eat up people, are those people.
Not our people, those people. I'm not saying who those
people are, whoever fits "those." And usually they end
up trying to put all those characteristics on us to hide
their own guilt. They shouldn't do that. It should be
emphasized over and over and over by you and me
that we aren't racists. One of the worst categories to
let them put you in is the category of racist.

I'm not a racist. I don't judge a man because of his
color. I get suspicious of a lot of them and cautious
around a lot of them — from experience. Not because
of their color, but because of what experience has taught
me concerning their overall behavior toward us. So,
please don't ever go away saying that we are against
people because of their color. We are against them because of what they *do* to us and because of what they
do to others. All they have to do to get our good will
is to show their good will and stop doing all those dirty
things to our people. Is that understood?

Also, within the next couple of weeks we will spell out

the type of support we got on our effort to bring the United States into the United Nations and charge her with violating our human rights. You and I *must* take this government before a world forum and show the world that this government has absolutely failed in its duty toward us. It has failed from Washington, D. C., all the way in to New York City. They have failed in their duty toward you and me. They have failed to protect us, they have failed to represent us, they have failed to respect us. And since they have failed, either willingly or because of their inability, we think that they should be brought up there so the world can see them as they actually are.

Now, if this government doesn't want to have her linen washed in public, then we give her a week or two to get her house in order. And if she can't get it in order in two weeks, then get on out there with South Africa and Portugal and the rest of those criminals who have been exploiting and abusing dark-skinned people now for far too long. We're all fed up. Right? Right.

[*Malcolm introduces Jesse Gray, who suggests that the place to send black mercenaries is Mississippi, and concludes: "It's always very easy for us to be ready to move and ready to talk and ready to act, but unless we truly get down into the heart of the ghetto and begin to deal with the problems of jobs, schools, and the other basic questions, we are going to be unable to deal with any revolutionary perspective, or with any revolution for that matter." Malcolm then says:*]

That was our brother Jesse Gray, the leader of the Harlem rent strikes, and what he said is true. When I speak of some action for the Congo, that action also includes Congo, Mississippi. But the point and thing that I would like to impress upon every Afro-American leader is that there is no kind of action in this country ever going to bear fruit unless that action is tied in with the overall international struggle.

You waste your time when you talk to this man, just you and him. So when you talk to him, let him know your brother is behind you, and you've got some more brothers behind that brother. That's the only way to talk to him, that's the only language he knows. Why do I say, "Make sure your brother is behind you"? Because you're going to have to fight this man, believe me, yes, *you're going to have to fight him.* You're going to have to fight him. He doesn't know any other language.

You can go and talk that old pretty talk to him, he doesn't even hear you. He says yes, yes, yes. You know, you can't communicate if one man is speaking French and the other one is speaking German. They've both got to speak the same language. Well, in this country you're dealing with a man who has a language. Find out what that language is. Once you know what language he speaks in, then you can talk to him. And if you want to know what his language is, study his history. His language is blood, his language is power, his language is brutality, his language is everything that's brutal.

And if you can't talk that talk, he doesn't even hear you. You can come talking that old sweet talk, or that old peace talk, or that old nonviolent talk—that man doesn't hear that kind of talk. He'll pat you on your back and tell you you're a good boy and give you a peace prize. How are you going to get a peace prize when the war's not over yet? I'm for peace, but the only way you're going to preserve peace is be prepared for war.

Never let anybody tell you and me the odds are against us—I don't even want to hear that. Those who think the odds are against you, forget it. The odds are not against you. The odds are against you only when you're scared. The only things that makes odds against you is a scared mind. When you get all of that fright off of you, there's no such thing as odds against you. Because when a man knows that when he starts playing with you, he's got to kill you, that man is not going to play with you. But if he knows when he's playing with you that you're going to back up and be nonviolent and peaceful and respectable and responsible, why, you and me will never come out of his claws.

Let him know that you're peaceful, let him know that you're respectful and you respect him, and that you're law-abiding, and that you want to be a good citizen, and all those right-thinking things. But let him know at the same time that you're ready to do to him what he's been trying to do to you. And then you'll always have peace. You'll always have it. Learn a lesson from history, learn a lesson from history.

I must say this once before we close. I don't want you to think that I'm coming back here to rabble-rouse, or to get somebody excited. I don't think you have to excite our people; the man already has excited us. And I don't want you to think that I'm ready for some unintelligent action, or some irresponsible action, or for just any old thing just to be doing something. No. I hope that all of us can sit down with a cool head and a clear mind and analyze the situation, in the back room, anywhere, analyze the situation; and after we give the proper analysis of what we're confronted by, then let us be bold enough to take whatever steps that analysis says must be taken. Once we get it, then let's do it, and we'll be able to get some kind of result in this freedom struggle.

But don't let anybody who is oppressing us ever lay the ground rules. Don't go by their game, don't play the game by their rules. Let them know now that this is a new game, and we've got some new rules, and these rules mean anything goes, *anything goes*. Are you with me, brothers? I know you're with me.

So, again I thank you and we will look for all of you out here, if possible, two weeks from tonight on the 13th of December. By the way, I want to tell you, I was in Paris Monday night before Alioune Diop's group, Présence Africaine. Many of our people in Paris, as well as from the African continent, are organizing, and they are just as concerned with what is going on over here as you and I are. You and I have to link up with our people who are in Paris — when I say our people, you know, *us* — we have to link up with our people who are in London, England. We've got a whole lot of them over there, brothers, I saw them.

We've got to link up with our people who are in the
Caribbean, in Trinidad, in Jamaica, in all the islands,
and we've got to link up with our people who are in
Central America and South America. Everywhere you
see someone who looks like us, we've got to get together.
And once we get together, brothers, we can get some
action, because we'll find we are not the underdog. All
those odds this man's talking about don't exist. He
put them in our minds—right or wrong? Very good.
So we thank you, and we'll see you in two weeks. May
Allah bless you.

THE YOUNG
10 SOCIALIST INTERVIEW

The following interview was granted by Malcolm X on January 18, 1965, to Jack Barnes and Barry Sheppard, representatives of the Young Socialist Alliance. After being transcribed and slightly shortened, the text was shown to Malcolm, who expressed satisfaction with the way it had been edited. It is reprinted from Young Socialist, *March-April, 1965.*

The most significant part of this interview was Malcolm's answer to the question asking how he defined black nationalism. It showed that Malcolm had been grappling with the problem of black nationalism — not in the sense of rejecting it, but of reappraising it, in order to discover how it fitted into his overall philosophy and strategy. It is additional evidence that even in the last month of his life he continued, despite the pressures he felt closing in on him, to think and rethink the problems confronting the black liberation movement, and that he was not ashamed to admit he didn't yet have all the answers he was seeking.

Question: What image of you has been projected by the press?

Malcolm X: Well, the press has purposely and skillfully projected me in the image of a racist, a race supremacist, and an extremist.

Question: What's wrong with this image? What do you really stand for?

Malcolm: First, I'm not a racist. I'm against every form of racism and segregation, every form of discrimination. I believe in human beings, and that all human beings should be respected as such, regardless of their color.

Question: Why did you break with the Black Muslims?

Malcolm: I didn't break, there was a split. The split came about primarily because they put me out, and they put me out because of my uncompromising approach to problems I thought should be solved and the movement could solve.

I felt the movement was dragging its feet in many areas. It didn't involve itself in the civil or civic or political struggles our people were confronted by. All it did was stress the importance of moral reformation — don't drink, don't smoke, don't permit fornication and adultery. When I found that the hierarchy itself wasn't practicing what it preached, it was clear that this part of its program was bankrupt.

So the only way it could function and be meaningful in the community was to take part in the political and economic facets of the Negro struggle. And the organization wouldn't do that because the stand it would have to take would have been too militant, uncompromising, and activist, and the hierarchy had gotten conservative. It was motivated mainly by protecting its own self interests. I might also point out that although the Black Muslim movement professed to be a religious group, the religion they had adopted — Islam — didn't recognize them. So, religiously it was in a vacuum. And it didn't take part in politics, so it was not a political group. When you have an organization that's neither political nor religious and doesn't take part in the civil rights struggle, what

can it call itself? It's in a vacuum. So, all of these factors led to my splitting from the organization.
Question: What are the aims of your new organization?
Malcolm: There are two organizations — there's the Muslim Mosque, Inc., which is religious. Its aim is to create
an atmosphere and facilities in which people who are
interested in Islam can get a better understanding of Islam. The aim of the other organization, the Organization of Afro-American Unity, is to use whatever means
necessary to bring about a society in which the 22 million
Afro-Americans are recognized and respected as human
beings.
Question: How do you define black nationalism, with
which you have been identified?
Malcolm: I used to define black nationalism as the
idea that the black man should control the economy of
his community, the politics of his community, and so
forth.
But, when I was in Africa in May, in Ghana, I was
speaking with the Algerian ambassador who is extremely militant and is a revolutionary in the true sense of
the word (and has his credentials as such for having
carried on a successful revolution against oppression in
his country). When I told him that my political, social,
and economic philosophy was black nationalism, he
asked me very frankly, well, where did that leave him?
Because he was white. He was an African, but he was
Algerian, and to all appearances, he was a white man.
And he said if I define my objective as the victory of
black nationalism, where does that leave him? Where
does that leave revolutionaries in Morocco, Egypt, Iraq,
Mauritania? So he showed me where I was alienating
people who were true revolutionaries dedicated to overturning the system of exploitation that exists on this
earth by any means necessary.
So, I had to do a lot of thinking and reappraising
of my definition of black nationalism. Can we sum up
the solution to the problems confronting our people as
black nationalism? And if you notice, I haven't been
using the expression for several months. But I still would

be hard pressed to give a specific definition of the overall philosophy which I think is necessary for the liberation of the black people in this country.

Question: Is it true, as is often said, that you favor
violence?

Malcolm: I don't favor violence. If we could bring
about recognition and respect of our people by peaceful means, well and good. Everybody would like to
reach his objectives peacefully. But I'm also a realist.
The only people in this country who are asked to be
nonviolent are black people. I've never heard anybody
go to the Ku Klux Klan and teach them nonviolence,
or to the Birch society and other right-wing elements.
Nonviolence is only preached to black Americans and
I don't go along with anyone who wants to teach our
people nonviolence until someone at the same time is
teaching our enemy to be nonviolent. I believe we should
protect ourselves by any means necessary when we are
attacked by racists.

Question: What do you think is responsible for race
prejudice in the U. S.?

Malcolm: Ignorance and greed. And a skillfully
designed program of miseducation that goes right along
with the American system of exploitation and oppression.

If the entire American population were properly educated — by properly educated, I mean given a true picture of the history and contributions of the black man —
I think many whites would be less racist in their feelings.
They would have more respect for the black man as a
human being. Knowing what the black man's contributions to science and civilization have been in the past, the
white man's feelings of superiority would be at least partially negated. Also, the feeling of inferiority that the
black man has would be replaced by a balanced knowledge of himself. He'd feel more like a human being.
He'd function more like a human being, in a society of
human beings.

So it takes education to eliminate it. And just because
you have colleges and universities, doesn't mean you
have education. The colleges and universities in the Amer-

ican educational system are skillfully used to miseducate.
Question: What were the highlights of your trip to
Africa?

Malcolm: I visited Egypt, Arabia, Kuwait, Lebanon,
Sudan, Ethiopia, Kenya, Tanganyika, Zanzibar (now
Tanzania), Nigeria, Ghana, Liberia, Guinea and Algeria. During that trip I had audiences with President
Nasser of Egypt, President Nyerere of Tanzania, President Jomo Kenyatta (who was then Prime Minister)
of Kenya, Prime Minister Milton Obote of Uganda,
President Azikiwe of Nigeria, President Nkrumah of
Ghana, and President Sékou Touré of Guinea. I think
the highlights were the audiences I had with those persons
because it gave me a chance to sample their thinking.
I was impressed by their analysis of the problem, and
many of the suggestions they gave went a long way
toward broadening my own outlook.

Question: How much influence does revolutionary Africa have on the thinking of black people in this country?

Malcolm: All the influence in the world. You can't
separate the militancy that's displayed on the African
continent from the militancy that's displayed right here
among American blacks. The positive image that is
developing of Africans is also developing in the minds
of black Americans, and, consequently they develop a
more positive image of themselves. Then they take more
positive steps — actions.

So you can't separate the African revolution from
the mood of the black man in America. Neither could
the colonization of Africa be separated from the menial
position that the black man in this country was satisfied
to stay in for so long. Since Africa has gotten its independence through revolution, you'll notice the stepped-
up cry against discrimination that has appeared in the
black community.

Question: How do you view the role of the U. S. in
the Congo?

Malcolm: As criminal. Probably there is no better example of criminal activity against an oppressed people
than the role the U. S. has been playing in the Congo,

through her ties with Tshombe and the mercenaries. You can't overlook the fact that Tshombe gets his money from the U. S. The money he uses to hire these mercenaries — these paid killers imported from South Africa — comes from the United States. The pilots that fly these planes have been trained by the U. S. The bombs themselves that are blowing apart the bodies of women and children come from the U. S. So I can only view the role of the United States in the Congo as a criminal role. And I think the seeds she is sowing in the Congo she will have to harvest. The chickens that she has turned loose over there have got to come home to roost.

Question: What about the U. S. role in South Vietnam?

Malcolm: The same thing. It shows the real ignorance of those who control the American power structure. If France, with all types of heavy arms, as deeply entrenched as she was in what then was called Indochina, couldn't stay there, I don't see how anybody in their right mind can think the U. S. can get *in* there — it's impossible. So it shows her ignorance, her blindness, her lack of foresight and hindsight and her complete defeat in South Vietnam is only a matter of time.

Question: How do you view the activity of white and black students who went to the South last summer and attempted to register black people to vote?

Malcolm: The attempt was good — I should say the objective to register black people in the South was good because the only real power a poor man in this country has is the power of the ballot. But I don't believe sending them in and telling them to be nonviolent was intelligent. I go along with the effort toward registration but I think they should be permitted to use whatever means at their disposal to defend themselves from the attacks of the Klan, the White Citizens Council and other groups.

Question: What do you think of the murder of the three civil rights workers and what's happened to their killers?

Malcolm: It shows that the society we live in is not actually what it tries to represent itself as to the rest of the world. This was murder and the federal govern-

ment is helpless because the case involves Negroes. Even
the whites involved, were involved in helping Negroes.
And concerning anything in this society involved in helping Negroes, the federal government shows an inability
to function. But it can function in South Vietnam, in
the Congo, in Berlin and in other places where it has
no business. But it can't function in Mississippi.

Question: In a recent speech you mentioned that you
met John Lewis of SNCC in Africa. Do you feel that
the younger and more militant leaders in the South
are broadening their views on the whole general struggle?

Malcolm: Sure. When I was in the Black Muslim movement I spoke on many white campuses and black campuses. I knew back in 1961 and 1962 that the younger
generation was much different from the older, and that
many students were more sincere in their analysis of the
problem and their desire to see the probelm solved. In
foreign countries the students have helped bring about
revolution — it was the students who brought about the
revolution in the Sudan, who swept Syngman Rhee out
of office in Korea, swept Menderes out in Turkey. The
students didn't think in terms of the odds against them,
and they couldn't be bought out.

In America students have been noted for involving themselves in panty raids, goldfish swallowing, seeing how
many can get in a telephone booth — not for their revolutionary political ideas or their desire to change unjust
conditions. But some students are becoming more like
their brothers around the world. However, the students
have been deceived somewhat in what's known as the
civil rights struggle (which was never designed to solve
the problem). The students were maneuvered in the direction of thinking the problem was already analyzed, so
they didn't try to analyze it for themselves.

In my thinking, if the students in this country forgot
the analysis that has been presented to them, and they
went into a huddle and began to research this problem
of racism for themselves, independent of politicians and
independent of all the foundations (which are a part
of the power structure), and did it themselves, then some

of their findings would be shocking, but they would
see that they would never be able to bring about a solution to racism in this country as long as they're rely-
ing on the government to do it. The federal government
itself is just as racist as the government in Mississippi,
and is more guilty of perpetuating the racist system.
At the federal level they are more shrewd, more skillful
at doing it, just like the FBI is more skillful than the
state police and the state police are more skillful than
the local police. The same with politicians. The politician
at the federal level is usually more skilled than the politician at the local level, and when he wants to practice
racism, he's more skilled in the practice of it than those
who practice it at the local level.

Question: What is your opinion of the Democratic Party?

Malcolm: The Democratic Party is responsible for the
racism that exists in this country, along with the Republican Party. The leading racists in this country are Democrats. Goldwater isn't the leading racist—he's a racist
but not the leading racist. The racists who have influence
in Washington, D. C., are Democrats. If you check, whenever any kind of legislation is suggested to mitigate the
injustices that Negroes suffer in this country, you will
find that the people who line up against it are members
of Lyndon B. Johnson's party. The Dixiecrats are Democrats. The Dixiecrats are only a subdivision of the Democratic party, and the same man over the Democrats is
over the Dixiecrats.

Question: What contribution can youth, especially students, who are disgusted with racism in this society, make
to the black struggle for freedom?

Malcolm: Whites who are sincere don't accomplish anything by joining Negro organizations and making them
integrated. Whites who are sincere should organize among
themselves and figure out some strategy to break down
the prejudice that exists in white communities. This is
where they can function more intelligently and more
effectively, in the white community itself, and this has
never been done.

Question: What part in the world revolution are youth

playing, and what lessons may this have for American youth?

Malcolm: If you've studied the captives being caught by the American soldiers in South Vietnam, you'll find that these guerrillas are young people. Some of them are just children and some haven't reached their teens. Most are teenagers. It is the teenagers abroad, all over the world, who are actually involving themselves in the struggle to eliminate oppression and exploitation. In the Congo, the refugees point out that many of the Congolese revolutionaries are children. In fact, when they shoot captive revolutionaries, they shoot all the way down to seven years old—that's been reported in the press. Because the revolutionaries are children, young people. In these countries, the young people are the ones who most quickly identify with the struggle and the necessity to eliminate the evil conditions that exist. And here in this country, it has been my own observation that when you get into a conversation on racism and discrimination and segregation, you will find young people more incensed over it—they feel more filled with an urge to eliminate it.

I think young people here can find a powerful example in the young *Simbas* in the Congo and the young fighters in South Vietnam.

Another point—as the dark-skinned nations of this earth become independent, as they develop and become stronger, that means that time is on the side of the American Negro. At this point the American Negro is still hospitable and friendly and forgiving. But if he is continually tricked and deceived and so on, and if there is still no solution to his problems, he will become completely disillusioned, disenchanted, and dissociate himself from the interest of America and its society. Many have done that already.

Question: What is your opinion of the worldwide struggle now going on between capitalism and socialism?

Malcolm: It is impossible for capitalism to survive, primarily because the system of capitalism needs some blood to suck. Capitalism used to be like an eagle, but

now it's more like a vulture. It used to be strong enough
to go and suck anybody's blood whether they were strong
or not. But now it has become more cowardly, like the
vulture, and it can only suck the blood of the helpless.
As the nations of the world free themselves, then capitalism has less victims, less to suck, and it becomes weaker
and weaker. It's only a matter of time in my opinion
before it will collapse completely.

Question: What is the outlook for the Negro struggle
in 1965?

Malcolm: Bloody. It was bloody in 1963, it was bloody
in 1964, and all of the causes that created this bloodshed
still remain. The March on Washington was designed
to serve as a vent or valve for the frustration that produced this explosive atmosphere. In 1964 they used the
Civil Rights bill as a valve. What can they use in 1965?
There is no trick that the politicians can use to contain
the explosiveness that exists right here in Harlem. And
look at New York Police Commissioner Murphy. He's
coming out in headlines trying to make it a crime now
to even predict that there's going to be trouble. This
shows the caliber of American thinking. There's going
to be an explosion, but don't talk about it. All the ingredients that produce explosions exist, but don't talk
about it, he says. That's like saying 700 million Chinese
don't exist. This is the same approach. The American
has become so guilt-ridden and filled with fear that instead of facing the reality of any situation he pretends
the situation doesn't exist. You know, in this country
it's almost a crime to say there's a place called China —
unless you mean that little island called Formosa. By
the same token, it's almost a crime to say that people in
Harlem are going to explode because the social dynamite
that existed last year is still here. So I think 1965 will
be most explosive — more explosive than it was in 1964
and 1963. There's nothing they can do to contain it.
The Negro leaders have lost their control over the people.
So that when the people begin to explode — and their
explosion is justified, not unjustified — the Negro leaders
can't contain it.

11
ON BEING
BARRED FROM FRANCE

Two weeks before his death, Malcolm X went to London to address the first congress of the Council of African Organizations. From London he was scheduled to fly to Paris to speak before the Congress of African Students. But when his plane landed at Orly on February 9, 1965, Malcolm was told he could not disembark. Later that day, back in London, he gave the following interview by telephone to a supporter of the meeting he was to have addressed in Paris (reprinted from The Militant, *February 20, 1967).*

After Malcolm was assassinated at the Audubon Ballroom in New York on February 21, 1965, some of his associates expressed the belief that the French government had excluded him earlier in the month because it thought that he might be assassinated on French soil, and did not want to bear the onus of such a scandal.

Eric Norden, a freelance journalist, wrote in The Realist *(February, 1967): "This assumption is more than idle speculation. In April, 1965 my interest in Malcolm's death was first aroused by a highly-placed North African*

167

*diplomat. This official, who insists on anonymity, said
that his country's intelligence department had been quiet-
ly informed by the French Department of Alien Docu-
mentation and Counter-Espionage that the CIA planned
Malcolm's murder, and France feared he might be liqui-
dated on its soil. . . 'Your CIA is beginning to murder
its own citizens now,' he commented in elegantly modu-
lated French."*

Question: Malcolm, Malcolm, how are you? A whole lot
of people turned out at the airport to meet you, and we
saw you leaving and we just called off the meeting tonight—what, you don't think we should have?

Malcolm X: No, go ahead and have it.

Question: You say go ahead and have it? Good. How
are you, brother? Look, brother, we're taping this so
give us a statement. Just talk.

Malcolm: I was surprised when I turned up at Paris
and got off the plane and was arrested. I thought if
there was any country in Europe that was liberal in its
approach to things, France was it, so I was shocked when
I got there and I couldn't land. They wouldn't even give
me any excuse or explanation. At first I thought it was
the American State Department. The only answer seemed
to be that France had become a satellite of Washington,
D. C.

In fact I've been all over the world—and I've been
in Alabama and Mississippi—and it's the first time in
my life that I was ever stopped outright. They wouldn't
give me any explanation whatsoever, nor would they
permit me to telephone to my friends there in Paris,
nor would they permit me to telephone to the American
embassy.

I asked the allowance of telephoning the American
embassy and they wouldn't even do that, and gave me
the impression that it was the embassy that had asked
them not to let me in. They kept trying to hint that it
was the American embassy in order to put the weight
off themselves.

And I might point out, I didn't think it would happen

in Paris. So as I told the security forces there, if I had
gone to South Africa or Johannesburg, or some place
where racism is practiced openly by the government,
I would not have been surprised, but to see a French
official representing a government that is supposedly
liberal, treating me in a worse way than I would be
treated if I went to South Africa, and taking into consideration the fact that Tshombe, a cold-blooded murderer and despot of the worst sort, was admitted to come
to France. He was entertained by the French government. And every other lowdown type of person has
been permitted to come to France.

And I frankly believe that if the people in France permit
that type of government to continue to exist that it will
humiliate them and disgrace them and embarrass them
all over the world. So, you know, I gave the security
forces there a penny, an English penny, you know, and
told them to give this to de Gaulle, because from my
point of view, his government and country were worth
less than one penny.

Question: Tell me, do you feel that the United States
government definitely has something to do with this?
What do you feel about that?

Malcolm: Well, you know I can't really understand . . .
when I asked someone today to call the American embassy and the American embassy put out a statement
[*unclear on tape*] they couldn't do anything about it,
where at the same time the same American embassy
was willing to send troops into the Congo to rescue
a man named Carlson who was not even a diplomat
but one of the missionaries there. They can do something about that. The same American embassy has troops
in South Vietnam and they can do whatever they want
to do all over the world, but when at the same time
they can't do something about the mishandling of a black
man, then I think something is wrong.

Whether or not the embassy — they had a hand in giving direct orders to the French government, I don't know.

Question: I see, brother. What do you think will be
the reaction in the nonwhite world, mainly the African
countries, towards the action of the French government?

Malcolm: Well, I don't know — already as you know I had been in London the night before addressing the first congress of the Council of African Organizations, and when I got back to London, there were representatives of about fifteen different African organizations waiting for me at the airport because they thought I had met with foul play, and they were getting ready to demonstrate. Now what I do know quite certainly: I have already been told that a protest will be launched throughout the European continent and elsewhere around the world in regard to this very criminal and uncouth action on the part of the French government.

Well, did they give you any explanation over there?

Question: Well, the French newspapers have come out this evening saying that the French government did it because of the fact that the speech you gave here in November was too "violent." It's quite ironical, you know, because that was one of the most moderate . . .

However right now we're getting ready to call the meeting for tonight. And we're taping your speech right now on the phone because we would like you to speak tonight at the meeting. They are not going to frustrate our plans.

Malcolm: Just let the meeting go ahead.

I do not advocate violence, in fact the violence that exists in the United States is the violence that the Negro in America has been a victim of and I have never advocated our people going out and initiating any acts of aggression against whites indiscriminately.

But I do say that the Negro is a continual victim of the violent actions committed by the organized elements like the Ku Klux Klan and if the United States government has shown itself unwilling or unable to protect us and our lives and our property, I have said that is time for our people to organize and band together and protect ourselves, to defend ourselves against this violence. Now if that is to advocate violence, then I'm shocked at the lack of proper understanding on the part of whatever elements over there that have this attitude.

Also there are those that have accused me of being a racist. I am not a racist in any way, shape or form,

and I believe in taking an uncompromising stand against
any forms of segregation and discrimination that are
based on race. I, myself, do not judge a man by the
color of his skin. The yardstick that I use to judge a
man is his deeds, his behavior, his intentions. And the
press has very skillfully projected me in the image of
a racist simply because I take an uncompromising stand
against the racism that exists in the United States. I think
it is an injustice, not only to me, but to the French public,
or whatever public, that is being misled in this way
by the press, especially at a time when efforts are being
made by well-meaning people to bring the various racial
sections together in trying to create an atmosphere of
better understanding.

So by and large, I think the only way of solving our
problems is to realize that people we think are liberal
are not as liberal as they profess; and people we think
are with us, when we put them to the test, they are not
really with us, they are not really for the oppressed
people as we think. And I hope the Afro-American community in Paris, as well as in other parts of Europe,
will realize the importance of us sticking together in
unity and brotherhood and doing something to solve
our own problems, and if there are well-meaning whites
also who are interested in helping, I think they should
realize we will accept their help too, but the attitude of
many elements makes it doubtful as to the sincerity
of those who profess to want to help.

Question: You say you were in London, brother, before coming to Paris. What were you doing in London?

Malcolm: Well, I came to London on the invitation
of the Council of African Organizations, with headquarters here in London. They were giving a congress,
the first congress, and there were a series of seminars
dealing with the African revolution.

They invited me here to describe to them the rate of
progress being made by black Americans in our struggle for human rights, and they also invited me to describe to them the stage or type of race relations that
exists between the black and white Americans and wheth-

er or not progress has been made in race relations. And
I think they showed their interest in the brothers and
sisters there on the American continent by inviting an
Afro-American to this congress and to bring them up
to date. I came to Paris this morning for this purpose
and I was going to try to convey the same message.

Question: What is the situation like in the United States,
Brother Malcolm? You were in Selma?

Malcolm: Yes, I was in Selma last Wednesday. I was
invited to the Tuskegee Institue and spoke before 3,000
black students on Tuesday night and they insisted I
go to Selma next morning. I went there. I saw the Ku
Klux Klan and other elements parading there. And I
saw one little girl called Judy [*unclear*] who was about
12 years old whom they arrested and [*unclear*] . . .
morning they told me how they were brutally treating
her in jail and how they took those cattle prods and
put them to her head and she was [*unclear*] . . .

So the treatment of black people in Selma, Alabama,
is extremely brutal, but what I understand is that Dr.
Martin Luther King got out of jail and wanted to go
to Washington, D. C., to see Lyndon B. to ask him for
some additional recognition concerning the voting rights
of Negroes. This, I fear, shows that the civil rights bill
that was passed last year means nothing because already now they are asking for new legislation, which
shows the [*unclear*] in their aims, and the sheer hypocrisy on the part of the government as regards the rights
of black people in the United States.

Question: Right, brother, and what are the prospects
for the struggle in the United States that you see for
this year?

Malcolm: Well, 1965 will probably be the longest, hottest, bloodiest summer that has yet been seen in the United
States since the beginning of the black revolution, primarily because the same causes that existed in the winter
of 1964 still exist in January—in February of 1965.
Now, these are causes of inferior housing, inferior employment, inferior education—all the evils of a bankrupt society still exist where black Americans are con-

cerned, and the resentment that exists has increased tre-
mendously, and now that the African nations themselves
have shown overt support for the black struggle in America and in our efforts to establish our human rights,
this gives us added incentive to step up our struggle,
and, as I said, 1965 will be the longest, hottest, bloodiest summer of the entire black revolution.

Question: We would like to know what do you think
the Afro-American community can do in the overall
struggle.

Malcolm: You mean the Afro-American community in
France?

Question: That's right, and in other parts of Europe.

Malcolm: The Afro-American community in France and
in other parts of Europe *must unite with the African
community*, and this was the message that I was going
to bring to Paris tonight—the necessity of the black
community in the Western Hemisphere, especially in the
United States and somewhat in the Caribbean area,
realizing once and for all that we must restore our cultural roots, we must establish contacts with our African
brothers, we must begin from this day forward to work
in unity and harmony as Afro-Americans along with
our African brothers.

(This) unity will give our struggle a type of strength
in spirit that will enable us to make some real concrete
progress whether we be in Europe, America, or on the
African continent. I wanted to show our brothers in
Paris the necessity of us forming a coalition, a *working*
community, with our brothers of the African continent.
Although the theme of my talk was the importance of
unity between the black people in the Western Hemisphere and those of the African continent, it was going
to be a regionalist approach—which I find is no different from what they have there in Europe, what they
call the European Common Market.

The European Common Market looks out for the common interests of Europeans and the European economy.
I feel it necessary for those of us who were taken from
the African continent and who today are suffering ex-

ploitation and oppression in the Western Hemisphere to reach out our hands and unite ourselves with our brothers and sisters again, wherever we are, and then work in unity and harmony for a positive program of mutual benefit.

Question: Unity — so that was the theme of your talk tonight, right? I would like to know what else you would have liked to have said to the African and Afro-American communities here in Paris?

Malcolm: My entire talk would have been based on the importance of unity, the unity between the . . .[*the tape cuts off*].

Question: Operator, operator!

Operator: Have you finished?

Question: No, we have not finished, operator.

Operator: Just a moment, you were cut off by the switchboard.

Question: The switchboard? Hello! Hello! Why was the phone disconnected?

Operator: I don't know — it was cut off in the hotel . . .

Malcolm: Hello! I guess we better wind it up, brother.

Question: Yes, yes, brother. Then I would like to hear anything else you have to say to us.

Malcolm: Just the importance of unity, brothers.

Question: Well, fine, brother, thank you and you know our hearts, brother, our hearts, our souls, our bodies and minds are with you — you know we are but one.

Malcolm: Yes, I know that.

Question: This is the message that I, on behalf of the other brothers here in France would like to convey to you.

Woman's voice: And sisters.

12 SHORT STATEMENTS

The following is a selection of statements made by Malcolm X in various speeches, interviews and answers to questions during his last year. They are all printed here for the first time.

How We Got Here

Malcolm: You wouldn't be in this country if some enemy hadn't kidnapped you and brought you here. On the other hand, some of you think you came here on the *Mayflower.*

Group on Advanced Leadership meeting, Detroit, April 12, 1964

Fight or Forget It

Malcolm: I say bluntly that you have had a generation of Africans who actually believed that you could negotiate, negotiate, negotiate and eventually get some kind of independence. But you're getting a new generation that has been growing right now, and they're beginning to think with their own minds and see that you can't negotiate up on freedom nowadays. If something is yours by right, then fight for it or shut up. If you can't fight for it, then forget it.

London School of Economics, February, 1965

An Awkward World

Malcolm had told a fellow panelist on a radio discussion program, "You're in less trouble if you say

175

*Afro-American nowadays than if you say Negro," and
the panelist had replied that Afro-American, like Italian-
American and German-American, is an awkward phrase.*

Malcolm: Well, we're living in an awkward world. I
think the whole race problem has made relations in
America awkward. So you have to invent awkward
terms to describe the awkward situation.

Long John Nebel program, Station
WOR, New York, June 20, 1964

What They Mean by Violence

Malcolm: You're out of your mind if you don't think
that there's a racist element in the State Department.
I'm not saying that everybody in the State Department
is a racist, but I'm saying they've sure got some in
there — a whole lot of them in there. They've got them
in powerful positions in there. This is the element that
became worried about the changing Negro mood and
the changing Negro behavior, especially if that mood
and that behavior became one of what they call violence.
By violence they only mean when a black man protects
himself against the attacks of a white man. This is what
they mean by violence. They don't mean what you mean.
Because they don't even use the word violence until
someone gives the impression that *you're* about to explode. When it comes time for a black man to explode
they call it violence. But white people can be exploding
against black people all day long, and it's never called
violence. I even have some of you come to me and ask
me, am I for violence? I'm the victim of violence, and
you're the victim of violence. But you've been so victim-
ized by it that you can't recognize it for what it is today.

HARYOU-ACT Forum, New York,
December 12, 1964

How to Get Allies

*Malcolm X went to England on December 3, 1964, to
participate in a debate sponsored by the Oxford Union*

Society and presented over television by the British Broadcasting Corporation. The question debated was "Extremism in the defense of liberty is no vice, moderation in the pursuit of justice is no virtue," a theme that had aroused heated controversy when it was propounded earlier in 1964 by Senator Barry Goldwater, the conservative Republican candidate for president. There were three speakers on each side, Malcolm being the final speaker for the affirmative. Despite continued efforts, we were unable to get more than a fragment of the transcript. (See also "Youth In a Time of Revolution," page 182 below.)

Malcolm: My reason for believing in extremism, intelligently directed extremism, extremism in defense of liberty, extremism in quest of liberty, is because I firmly believe in my heart that the day that the black man takes an uncompromising step and realizes that he's within his rights, when his own freedom is being jeopardized, to use any means necessary to bring about his freedom or put a halt to that injustice, I don't think he'll be by himself. I live in America where there are only 22 million blacks, against probably 160 million whites. One of the reasons why I'm in no way reluctant or hesitant to do whatever is necessary to see that blacks do something to protect themselves is I honestly believe that the day they do, many whites will have more respect for them, and there will be more whites on their side than are now on their side with these little wishy-washy love-thy-enemy approaches that they've been using up to now.

And if I'm wrong, then you are racialists.

> Oxford Union Society debate, December 3, 1964

Charges of Racism

Malcolm: If you noticed, the American press during the last week has been accusing the Africans in the United Nations of dealing in racism. Have you noticed that? Why? Because for the first time in the history of the UN every one of those foreign ministers or representatives

from Africa who come up there to speak on the Congo
question not only are speaking on the Congo but they're
talking about Mississippi and Alabama and New York
City. And you're going to find this, brothers, increasingly.

HARYOU-ACT Forum, New York,
December 12, 1964

Education

Malcolm: Without education, you are not going anywhere in this world.

Militant Labor Forum, New York,
May 29, 1964

Politics

Malcolm: Any time you throw your weight behind a
political party that controls two-thirds of the government,
and that party can't keep the promises that it made to
you during election time, and you're dumb enough to
walk around continuing to identify yourself with that
political party, you're not only a chump but you're a
traitor to your race.

Group on Advanced Leadership
meeting, Detroit, April 12, 1964

No Need To Be Vengeful

Malcolm: The 22 million Afro-Americans are not yet
filled with hate or the desire for vengeance as the propaganda of the segregationists would have you believe.
The universal law of justice is sufficient to bring judgment
upon those whites who are guilty of racism. It will also
punish those who have benefited from the racist practices
of their forefathers and done nothing to atone for them.
Most intelligent whites will admit without hesitation that
they are already being punished for the evil deeds committed against the Afro-Americans by their fathers. Thus
it is not necessary for the victim — the Afro-American —

to be vengeful. The very conditions that whites created are already plaguing them into insanity and death. They are reaping what they have sown. We, the 22 million Afro-Americans — the victims — will do better to spend our time removing the scars from our people, scars left by 400 years of inhuman treatment in America.

Chicago debate, May 23, 1964

The Role of Women

Malcolm's views on the role and place of women underwent considerable change in his last year, especially after his second trip to Africa in 1964, when he began to consider the question not in traditional moral terms but from the standpoint of mobilizing the forces needed to revolutionize society. The following remarks, made after the second African trip, are in marked contrast to those about women that appear in the Autobiography:

Malcolm: One thing that I became aware of in my traveling recently through Africa and the Middle East, in every country you go to, usually the degree of progress can never be separated from the woman. If you're in a country that's progressive, the woman is progressive. If you're in a country that reflects the consciousness toward the importance of education, it's because the woman is aware of the importance of education. But in every backward country you'll find the women are backward, and in every country where education is not stressed it's because the women don't have education. So one of the things I became thoroughly convinced of in my recent travels is the importance of giving freedom to the woman, giving her education, and giving her the incentive to get out there and put that same spirit and understanding in her children. And I frankly am proud of the contributions that our women have made in the struggle for freedom and I'm one person who's for giving them all the leeway possible because they've made a greater contribution than many of us men.

Paris interview, November, 1964

Religion

Malcolm: This afternoon it's not our intention to talk religion. We're going to forget religion. If we bring up religion, we'll be in an argument. And the best way to keep away from arguments and differences, as I said earlier, is to put your religion at home, in the closet, keep it between you and your God. Because if it hasn't done anything more for you than it has, you need to forget it anyway.

Group on Advanced Leadership
meeting, Detroit, April 12, 1964

Whom to Fight

Malcolm: As long as we dilly-dally, and try to appear more moral than anybody else by taking a beating without fighting back, why, people will continue to refer to us as very moral persons and very well-disciplined persons, but at the same time we'll be just as far back a hundred years from now as we are today. So I believe that fighting against those who fight against us is the best course of action in any situation. Not fighting against anybody, but fighting against anybody who fights against us.

HARYOU-ACT Forum, New York,
December 12, 1964

Intellectuals and Socialism

Malcolm: In the past the Afro-American or American Negro intellectual perhaps permitted himself to be used in a way that wasn't really beneficial to the overall Afro-American struggle. But I think today these intellectuals have begun to undertake a new appraisal of the problem, are looking at it as it actually is, and are beginning to see it more in the intellectual context, the relation that it has with the African struggle. And the African intellectual is beginning to look at the problem in the African context and see that what might be good in one country, in order for it to be used in another country, has to be rearranged. You take African socialism. Many of the African intellectuals that have analyzed the approach of socialism are beginning to see where the African has to use a form of socialism that fits into the African context; whereas the form that is used in the European country might be good for that particular European country it doesn't fit as well into the African context. So I think the African intellectual is making that contribution and he's making it well.

Paris interview, November, 1964

A Master Hate-Teacher

Malcolm: Somebody's got nerve enough, some whites have the audacity, to refer to me as a hate teacher. If I'm teaching someone to hate, I'm teaching them to hate the Ku Klux Klan. But here and in America they have taught us to hate ourselves. To hate our skin, to hate our hair, to hate our features, hate our blood, hate what we are. Why, Uncle Sam is a master hate-teacher, so much so that he makes someone think he's teaching law when he's teaching hate. When you've made a man hate himself, you've really got it and gone.

London School of Economics, February, 1965

Here More than Abroad

Malcolm: If I understand you, you're saying that as this man, who at present is in places all over this earth where he doesn't belong, gets pushed out and comes back here where he *still* doesn't belong, will his dissatisfaction be so intense that he can't hide it any longer — is this what you're saying? — and then he will begin to show his real self? Well, he shows his real self here now more than he does when he's abroad. He probably will, brother, as times get tough abroad; it'll be more difficult for him to hide his hand, and his present indefensible position in the Congo is a sign of this. . . . When they

are brought back here from having been pushed out back
there, it is true that they have more animosity.

HARYOU-ACT Forum, New York,
December 12, 1964

Youth in a Time of Revolution

Malcolm: I don't believe in any form of unjustified extremism, but I believe that when a man is exercising
extremism, a human being is exercising extremism, in
defense of liberty for human beings, it's no vice. And
when one is moderate in the pursuit of justice for human
beings, I say he's a sinner. And I might add in my
conclusion—in fact, America is one of the best examples,
when you read its history, about extremism. Old Patrick
Henry said "liberty or death"—that's extreme, very extreme.

I read once, passingly, about a man named
Shakespeare—I only read about him passingly, but I
remember one thing he wrote that kind of moved me.
He put it in the mouth of Hamlet, I think it was, who
said, "To be or not to be"—he was in doubt about something—"whether it was nobler in the mind to suffer the
slings and arrows of outrageous fortune"—moderation—
"or to take up arms against a sea of troubles, and by
opposing end them." And I go for that. If you take up
arms, you'll end it. But if you sit around and wait for
the one who's in power to make up his mind that he
should end it, you'll be waiting a long time.

And in my opinion the young generation of whites,
blacks, browns, whatever else there is, you're living
at a time of extremism, a time of revolution, a time
when there's got to be a change. People in power have
misused it, and now there has to be a change and a
better world has to be built, and the only way it's going
to be built is with extreme methods. I for one will join
in with anyone, I don't care what color you are, as long
as you want to change this miserable condition that
exists on this earth. Thank you.

Oxford Union Society debate, December 3, 1964

I'm a Field Negro

Malcolm: I have to say this, then I'll sit down. Back during slavery, when people like me talked to the slaves, they didn't kill them, they sent some old house Negro along behind him to undo what he said. You have to read the history of slavery to understand this.

There were two kinds of Negros. There was that old house Negro and the field Negro. And the house Negro always looked out for his master. When the field Negroes got too much out of line, he held them back in check. He put them back on the plantation.

The house Negro could afford to do that because he lived better than the field Negro. He ate better, he dressed better, and he lived in a better house. He lived right up next to his master — in the attic or the basement. He ate the same food as his master and wore his same clothes. And he could talk just like his master — good diction. And he loved his master more than his master loved himself. That's why he didn't want his master to get hurt.

If the master got hurt, he'd say: "What's the matter, boss, we sick?" When the master's house caught afire, he'd try and put out the fire. He didn't want his master's house burnt. He never wanted his master's property threatened. And he was more defensive of it than his master was. That was the house Negro.

But then you had some field Negroes, who lived in huts, had nothing to lose. They wore the worst kind of clothes. They ate the worst food. And they caught hell. They felt the sting of the lash. They hated this land.

You know what they did? If the master got sick, they'd pray that the master'd die. If the master's house caught afire, they'd pray for a strong wind to come along. This was the difference between the two.

And today you still have house Negroes and field Negroes.

I'm a field Negro. If I can't live in the house as a human being, I'm praying for a wind to come along. If the master won't treat me right and he's sick, I'll call the doctor to go in the other direction. But if all of us are going to live as human beings, then I'm for a society of human beings that can practice brotherhood.

But before I sit down, I want to thank you for listening to me. I hope I haven't put anybody on the spot. I'm not intending to try and stir you up and make you do something that you wouldn't have done anyway.

I pray that God will bless you in everything that you do. I pray that you will grow intellectually, so that you can understand the problems of the world and where you fit into that world picture. And I pray that all the fear that is evident in your heart will be taken out, and when you know that that man—if you know he's nothing but a coward, you won't fear him. If he wasn't a coward, he wouldn't gang up on you. This is how they function: They function in mobs—that's a coward. They put on a sheet so you won't know who they are—that's a coward.

Now the time will come when that sheet will be ripped off. If the federal government doesn't take it off, we'll take it off. Thank you.

Selma, Alabama, February 4, 1965

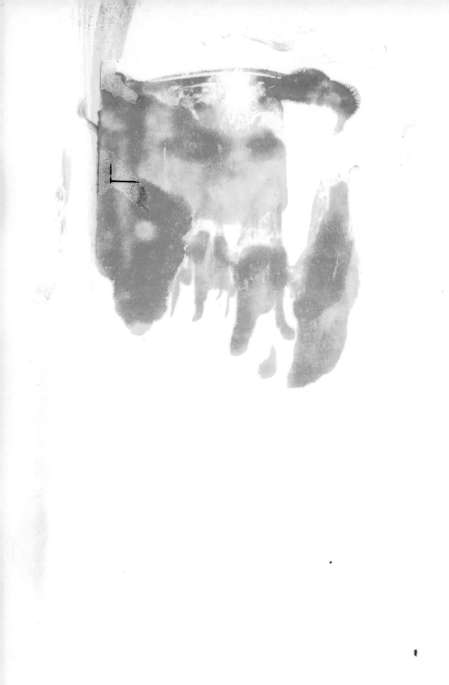